The
Uncapturable

ALSO AVAILABLE IN THE THEATRE MAKERS SERIES

The Uncapturable

The Fleeting Art of Theatre

Rubén Szuchmacher
Translated by
William Gregory

methuen | drama
LONDON • NEW YORK • OXFORD • NEW DELHI • SYDNEY

METHUEN DRAMA
Bloomsbury Publishing Plc
50 Bedford Square, London, WC1B 3DP, UK
1385 Broadway, New York, NY 10018, USA

BLOOMSBURY, METHUEN DRAMA and the Methuen Drama logo
are trademarks of Bloomsbury Publishing Plc

First published in Argentina 2015 as *Lo incapturable* by Reservoir Books
First published in Great Britain 2021

Work published within the framework of 'Sur' Translation Support Program of
the Ministry of Foreign Affairs, International Trade and Worship of the Argentine
Republic.

Obra editada en el marco del Programa 'Sur' de Apoyo a las Traducciones
del Ministerio de Relaciones Exteriores, Comercio Internacional y Culto de la
República Argentina.

Cover design: Charlotte Daniels
Cover image © Gustavo Gavotti

A catalogue record for this book is available from the British Library.

A catalog record for this book is available from the Library of Congress.

ISBN: HB: 978-1-3501-3885-8
         PB: 978-1-3501-3884-1
         ePDF: 978-1-3501-3886-5
         eBook: 978-1-3501-3887-2

Series: Theatre Makers

Typeset by Integra Software Services Pvt. Ltd.
Printed and bound in Great Britain

To find out more about our authors and books visit www.bloomsbury.com
and sign up for our newsletters.

CONTENTS

ACKNOWLEDGEMENTS

To Graciela Schuster, because many of the ideas expressed in this book are thanks to the constant and daily work that we did together in the Talleres de Puesta en Escena (Mise en Scène Workshops). She generously showed me the paths to be able to think about the artistic from multiple perspectives.

To Jorge Ferrari, Gonzalo Córdova, Barbara Togander, Edgardo Rudnitzky, Ernesto Diz, Lautaro Vilo, Ingrid Pelicori, Horacio Peña and the late Cristina Moix, constant companions in my theatre work in design, lighting, music, acting and writing. They were not the only ones, but they are the ones who most left their mark on me.

To all my students at the Talleres de Puesta en Escena, to those who agreed with me and those who did not.

To Laura Garaglia for her patient and passionate reading of these materials.

The writer and translator would like to express their particular thanks to Maria Delgado, Director of Research at The Royal Central School of Speech and Drama, for introducing them, and for her support for the the translation of this work into English.

You do look, my son, in a moved sort.
As if you were dismayed. Be cheerful, sir.
Our revels now are ended. These our actors,
As I foretold you, were all spirits and
Are melted into air, into thin air:
And, like the baseless fabric of this vision,
The cloud-capp'd towers, the gorgeous palaces,
The solemn temples, the great globe itself,
Yea, all which it inherit, shall dissolve
And, like this insubstantial pageant faded,
Leave not a rack behind. We are such stuff
As dreams are made on, and our little life
Is rounded with a sleep.

William Shakespeare, *The Tempest*

Introduction: object and action

For some time now, regular theatregoers in Argentina have observed how the following text can often be read in the programmes handed out before a performance:

Puesta en escena y dirección: ...

'Staging (or mise en scène) and direction', followed by someone's name.

It always surprises me to see the work of the person directing a show described in this way. Except for where the theatre culture is influenced by Argentina, most countries only use the words 'direction' or 'director' or some equivalent. It is fairly rare to find both 'mise en scène' and 'direction' used side by side.

Intrigued by this, I began asking colleagues – some of them experienced, but most of them fairly young, and more likely to use the twin term 'mise en scène and direction' – to describe their work: why this double naming? The replies were always similar. 'Mise en scène', they would say, refers to a show's aesthetics, while 'direction' describes the work with the actors.

Put like this, the distinction seems fairly logical. But if we dig a little deeper it soon proves inconsistent, for example, in its view that the work of the actors has nothing to do with the aesthetic questions pervading any piece of theatre. Meanwhile, in the jargon of theatre critics (and of many people working in Argentine theatre in general), it is thought that if directors concern themselves in any detail with the formal aspects of a show they cease to be a 'director' and become instead a *puestista* – a 'stager' – a title that is not highly valued.

In any work of theatre, the terms 'mise en scène' and 'direction' do indeed refer to two very different, albeit complementary things. But how exactly are these two ideas, always interlinked in any theatre practice, different to one another?

In that mise en scène is an *object*, while direction is an *action*. The mise en scène is the *resulting object* arising from the combination of *actions* carried out in the making of a show. An unstable object in constant flux, but an object nevertheless, and one produced by many people. From the actors to the technicians, from the set designer to the theatre maintenance team, from the playwright to the box office staff, all of them, each with their own distinct role, are responsible participants in the mise en scène or staging of a play.

And it is not only the work of the artists, technicians or administrators that is part of the mise en scène. It is also the space that houses the show, the production methods used and, above all, the audience members who attend the performances. For it is they who ultimately make sense of the whole operation.

Although it is sometimes hard to accept, *the mise en scène is an object that has no single owner*. For this reason it seems odd to read what we read in Argentine programmes: that someone called a 'director' could be the sole author of the mise en scène. Put like this, it amounts to one person taking undue credit for a collective endeavour.

Direction, on the other hand, is an action, a series of operations applied to a play's material – its strictly speaking theatrical elements – and which allows the mise en scène to be assembled in a more or less effective way.

Some of us may consider this action to be the most important element of the theatre system, the most *active* task as regards the intended course for this object in construction, because it sets out the general framework for a show's overall shape.

Although this action – as we will see later – may or may not necessarily be carried out by a person calling themselves a 'director', it has, in the majority of cases, one or several people directly responsible for it: all of those steering the collective task in hand on some kind of course.

This book addresses a number of questions relating to mise en scène and direction, to object and action. It considers the various elements involved in shaping something as complex as the performing arts, an art form whose products slip constantly through our fingers. Especially now, when the range of forms on offer on theatre bills throughout the world is so diverse, our understanding of theatre is becoming increasingly conflictive.

As Roland Barthes says, 'To write about something is to outmode it'.[1] Because of this I am still somewhat wary of stating any firm ideas about theatre. Doing so runs the risk of trying to turn the ideas discussed into universal, rock-solid truths, when in fact the performing arts are uncapturable.

Neither manual nor manifesto, this book is simply a collection of reflections, developed over years of intense theatre practice on many stages in various countries where I have met with the apprentices of the art of theatre. These thoughts are the results of these lived experiences, lived mainly as an actor and director, in text-based theatre, dance, musical theatre, opera and countless other tasks, among them the management of theatre spaces.

---

[1]Barthes, Roland, *A Lover's Discourse*, trans. Richard Howard (New York: Farrar, Straus & Giroux, 1978), p. 98.

PART ONE

The arts of the mise en scène

1.

When talking of the performing arts (also known as the scenic arts), which include any form involving a 'show' and an 'audience', be it theatre, dance or opera, there are often misunderstandings. The word 'theatre', especially, has a range of definitions so varied as to make it unlikely that those working in the field will ever agree on what it means.

Since the start of the twentieth century (that century which, as Eric Hobsbawn said, is 'the era of the most revolutionary transformations of human life so far recorded'[2]), performance practices across the planet have become so numerous and so different that, like in some modern Babel, it has become very difficult to know what is being talked about when speaking of 'theatre'.

Until the end of the nineteenth century, modes of performance developed over long periods of time. They also did so in exclusivity: there was only one way of making theatre, or at the most, two. Each era had its own, singular way of thinking about performance, and theatre-making practices were long-lasting and fairly homogeneous. The Greeks had their tragedies, comedies and theatre spaces, which could change in size but not in form. The tragedies could be better or worse, but the way of structuring them was always similar. In

---

[2]Hobsbawn, Eric, *Age of Extremes* (London: Abacus, 1994), p. 500.

other periods, when systems of theatrical production did change – for example, when Renaissance theatre shifted from performing on wagons or at inns to staging plays in proscenium arch theatres – these changes remained in place for centuries, until they themselves became another established system.

Since the beginning of the twentieth century, and with ever greater speed, many ways of making what is generically called 'theatre' have emerged and coexisted. There are immense venues for more than 10,000 people, and spaces for fewer than twenty; there are even shows made for an audience of one. There are end-on spaces, theatres in the round, traverse stages and promenade productions. There are purpose-built theatres and recycled spaces not originally intended for performance. All spaces from throughout theatre history are now available to artists and audiences alike. Greek theatres, Roman theatres, Elizabethan theatres, courtyard theatres, open-air theatres, theatres in underground bunkers and 1,001 types of proscenium arch.

There is theatre with actors trained at conservatoires and with people who work as actors but who have never set foot in a theatre school of any kind. Lighting systems range from the most complex to the most simple, sometimes with no transition in between. Design is no longer limited to wood and cloth, noble raw materials though they may be. Today, the industry offers the designer a vast array of materials. And not everything need be specially made: the use of real, pre-existing spaces, such as patios, houses, boats, hospitals and so on, as arenas for performance is an already established possible practice.

The starting point for a show can be a dramatic text by an author past or present, famous or unknown, but it may also be a non-dramatic text such as a novel, short story or instruction manual. It may be an undefined idea that develops through the work of the actors and the director. An enormous array of texts appear, not written at the desks of playwrights. And so too do new ways to produce them.

The barriers between genres and formats have now been lifted. Plays are not necessarily dramas, tragedies or comedies, as they once were. Combinations of theatre and dance, video and visual art are also the order of the day. In a theatre show, 'live' (onstage), 'deferred' (video projection) and 'remote' (online transmission) content can coexist.

Throughout the world, different forms of production exist: those produced by state-run theatres, commercial theatres, alternative or fringe venues, community groups and amateur companies. And lest we forget, today's theatregoer is much better informed than those in the past. Regardless of whether they go regularly to the theatre or not, the amount of visual, aural and literary information they receive in their homes through the television or via the internet has transformed audiences dramatically, and when they do attend a show they are increasingly demanding.

Today, the thing called theatre exists in a way that has spread across many spaces, in very different forms, appealing to very diverse audiences. It can be hard to know what all of these variations have *in common*. They may appear to have nothing similar about them, but there is still something that unites them and allows them still to be included under the same heading: the combined presence of multiple art forms – architecture, the visual arts, sound art and literature – within a single scenic object. For the art form we generically call 'theatre' to be made possible, these four art forms must invariably be joined together.

It was Adolphe Appia, one of the early twentieth century's greatest innovators of theatrical thought, who wrote about this union of the arts in his book, *The Work of Living Art*:

We have here a major art form that we can only refer to as such by placing the word 'art' before it. Why? First of all the extreme complexity of this form, resulting from the great number of media that it must make use of in order to manifest itself in a homogeneous way. Dramatic art is made up first of a text (with or without music); this is its literary (and musical) part. This text is entrusted to living beings who recite or sing it, representing life on the stage; this is its sculptural or painterly part [...] Finally, architecture may also be evoked to a lesser or greater extent around the author, or indeed around the audience, because the auditorium is also part of dramatic art, with its optical and acoustic demands [...] Thus dramatic art appears to borrow some elements from all of the other arts.[3]

---

[3]Appia, Adolphe, *L'oeuvre d'art vivant* (Geneva: Editions Atar, 1921). Translation for this volume by William Gregory.

Richard Wagner did this too, with his idea of the 'total work of art' (*Gesamtkunstwerk*), which thought of theatre – or in his case opera – as the intersection of the arts, an idea also taken up by Bertolt Brecht, albeit to debate it and to attempt to refute it. But beyond historical arguments about the presence of the arts within the scenic act, one thing is certain: whatever the kind of show – even in those with no artistic pretensions – all of them contain the same elements, arising from the different art forms that constitute them, and allowing the mise en scène to come into being.

2.

This *object, made up of four art forms (architecture, visual arts, sound art and literature) connected by a system of production, and with the aim of being received or watched, and which creates a fiction in a single time and space, is what I call the 'mise en scène'.* This definition includes not only all of theatre's possible forms, with its many ways of arranging its various materials (texts, images, mimesis), but also opera, musical theatre, dance, dance theatre and the vast etcetera expanding uncontrollably through the realm of the performing arts.

Each one of the art forms mentioned in this definition has a specific field of influence. Architecture establishes first and foremost the spatial relationship between the play and the audience; the visual arts refer to everything that the eye perceives physically; sound art, to everything that is heard and to the passing of time; and literature, to the recounting of narrative through words or movement. The interlinking of these four arts, as defined by a given system of production, takes place within an act in the present tense that is exhibited as *fiction*. To paraphrase Octave Mannoni, in his article 'The comic illusion or theatre from the point of view of the imaginary',[4] we can consider fiction to be present whenever a performance seeks to pass itself off as what it is not.

A mise en scène is a complex artistic object that only exists fully at the moment of encounter with an audience, in the same space and

---

[4]Mannoni, Octave, 'L'illusion comique ou le théâtre du point de vue de l'imaginaire', in *Clefs pour l'imaginaire* (Paris: Le Seuil, 1969).

at the same time. Not before the performance, not in the writing of the text, not in rehearsals, not at the technical rehearsal; nor after it is over, when the playtexts are published, nor in potential reviews in newspapers or magazines or on blogs, nor in a video of the show, nor in the memories of the audience or of the artists who were there at the time.

This absolute present makes the mise en scène very hard to create and very hard to analyse. Specifically, this difficulty lies in the impossibility of capturing this object which, *while it is happening* and once it is over, is not exactly an object, but *rather a trace of what it was.*

I want to stress that this combination of four art forms is part of any theatre act, regardless of the intended aesthetic or the place the show occupies in a community's cultural output. From the most lowbrow show to the most refined, from the most popular to the most 'elitist', wherever there is a mise en scène, it will be made up of this combination.

And these four art forms work together to make a whole. If any of these four elements are absent, the object created falls outside the realm of the performing arts.

If, when creating a mise en scène, any of the aforementioned art forms are left aside, we fall into a different artistic practice, no less legitimate, but distinct from an act of theatre.

For example, if literature is combined with visual art in any given space, fiction will likely result, such as in the well-known Book of Hours, *Les Très Riches Heures du Duc de Berry*, which combines the visual with narrative. But in this example there is no sound.

Similarly, a combination of sound and text may exist in a particular space, as in oratories or passions set to music. Here, there is narration, but it is not necessary to *see* what is happening in the place where the music is being played, because it is not necessary to see the visual aspects of the work in question (the musicians playing, the physical shapes that are present in the make-up of the orchestra etc.) in order to listen to it. In other words, there is fiction in the text, but not in the form of a play.

This simultaneous combination of four elements is also present in rock or pop concerts, and some people will no doubt describe these as mises en scène. But what they do not contain is fiction, even if a show uses a vast array of visual and sound devices. Despite the various costumes or the bizarre make-up, the show will not cease to be what it is: musicians playing to a group of listeners. Without fiction.

Where this definition of mise en scène can be seen most clearly is in the realm of *installations*. Here, the visual arts (and also sound art) flirt with the art of performance. Visual artists sometimes make objects that are called 'installations', but which have a single starting point and a single end point. In this case they would be classed as a mise en scène. On the other hand, there are some shows performed by actors or dancers that can only be defined as installations, because they have no set running time. In these cases, the works of art on show often fail to fulfil the stated intentions of the artists.

These four artistic disciplines intersecting within the mise en scène necessarily presuppose performers, be they actors, dancers, singers, musicians, puppets, and so forth. All of these are permeated by the architectural space, by the visual, by sound and by literature. Their bodies are large or small in relation to the space they move around in; they have a shape, because they are tall, short, fat or thin, and wear costumes of given colours; their voices are high, low, slow, fast, resonant or weak; and they inevitably tell some kind of story, with words or without them, with one action following another.

The mise en scène also assumes a given system of production, which connects these art forms and includes all of the people involved in making a piece of theatre: not only the actors, directors, designers, wardrobe designers, composers, choreographers, playwrights etc., but also all of a show's technical crew, such as stage hands, lighting and sound operators, props supervisors and so on, as well as a theatre's administrative and workshop staff. I add to this list those who make the programming decisions or those who fund the shows according to private or public policies, such as the directors of state-owned theatres or private producers. In other words, the system of production contains all of those who work on the creation of a mise en scène.

And finally, of course, the mise en scène also includes the audience, that collection of people who do not know each other and who gather in a space that is not theirs and that is very different to their own home. Even shows performed at private houses do not invalidate this statement. Experience shows that even this arena is reimagined as if it had no owner (even if it is owned) – that is to say, as if it were other to the audience – precisely because the space of fiction, the space of the play, overtakes the space of reality.

Every mise en scène shapes its audience, contains it and summons it. When some theatre artists declare that they do not take the spectator into account when they create, the truth is that these claims are more posturing than reality. In the performing arts this is impossible, precisely because, as I mentioned above, the mise en scène only exists in the final encounter with the audience. The play and the audience speak mutually to each other, making the existence of the theatrical possible.

Let us try to imagine a show without an audience. Just the artists on the stage, with no one in the seats watching them or listening to them. After a few performances they would in all likelihood each start to perform for their fellow performers, for the lighting operator or for the ushers. They would seek out an audience at any price, even inventing one in their heads.

We might think of the opposite: a group of spectators with no play. The same audience going every night to a theatre where there is no show. In this case, it is likely that one of them would start to 'act', to say a few lines they remember to entertain the others, to clown around and so forth. In other words, to take the place of the actors and to restore the place of the absent play. The emptiness of the stage is not only intolerable; it is also impossible.

Architecture

Space

Although many artists may state that the actor lies at the centre of the theatrical system, while others say it is the playwright, it is an unspoken truth that the starting point for any theatrical phenomenon is architecture. It is this that makes possible the existence of all of the other elements, since it allows for and shapes the very basis of the theatre: the indivisible union between play and audience.

When thinking about theatre architecture, we must therefore consider at least three possible areas:

1　The space of encounter between the play and the audience (theatre auditorium, enclosed hall or open air, on the street etc.)

2　The building or space that contains this meeting place, which is sometimes intended exclusively for this purpose but at other times is inserted into an establishment that has other uses as well as theatre (cultural centre, shopping centres, basements of apartment blocks etc.)

3　The position of this building or space within a particular community, that is to say its territorial location.

These three areas contain the necessary elements to allow us to redefine the idea of the *performance space*, a term that is often limited to the shape or use of the stage, leaving aside the space occupied by the audience. I suggest that the term be expanded to a broader definition, to include the architectural elements of theatre in all their various aspects, starting with the one that determines the relationship of the play with the audience. The notion of *performance space* would therefore include all of the areas where the performing arts take place.

First, the place where the play and the audience meet, a relationship that can take many different forms and that will have a fundamental effect on the mise en scène.

For most theatre artists, the theatre act takes place at a precise point between the playing space and the space of the audience. This event is not on one side or the other, but at the intersection of one *with* the other. It is in this indivisible place *between* the two spaces that the theatre act is created. But the elements contained in these two spaces (which in reality are one space divided into two, given that, invariably and regardless of the intentions of those on either side, there exists one playing space, which is the territory of fiction, and another space for the audience, which is the territory of non-fiction) determine all the possible configurations of the mise en scène. It is always worth clarifying that this is not about a fight between fiction and reality. The playing space is just as much 'reality' as the audience's; it is just that someone needs not to be fictional in order for the theatre act to exist at all. If everyone were part of the fiction, we would surely be in the realm of ritual, where there is no audience because everyone is a celebrant.

Dimensions such as the height, length and width of both the playing space and the audience area; the overall volume of the space; the colour of the audience area and sometimes of the playing space (whose coloured or textured features may become part of the performance even despite themselves); the various ornamentations; the technology used in the playing space and also in the audience space (like the arrangement of lighting equipment, and so on), are the *unavoidable physical reality* that determines not only the make-up of the play but also the possible ways it may be received by the audience.

This meeting place is generally contained within another place, the theatre building, that is to say a larger area that contains this other particular space. The theatre 'building' may be a closed or open-air space; it makes no difference. The concept of a 'building' does not refer exclusively to the idea of solid materials or closed spaces, but rather to the construction of a border that holds the playing space–audience space relationship within it and, by extension, protects the two parties involved. This is obvious in a building, be it theatrical or not, but it is also obvious in an open-air space, be it a square or a street or any other area that has not been conceived especially for theatre. It becomes necessary to delineate a space inside another space, to act as a defence against the leakage that takes place in spaces that are not enclosed. In most cases this *border*, this 'construction of a theatre building', is carried out by the bodies of the audience themselves, for example, surrounding a street performance. They protect it, creating a human wall and isolating it from the rest of the space so that the performance can take place with as little outside interference as possible.

Like Russian dolls, the third element of theatre architecture is *the position* of a particular place in a community where the theatre building – which in turn contains this other space of relationship between the play and the audience – is located. The 'meaning' or 'value' of a building may vary from one community to another. The location of a performance space in a certain part of a city will also affect the response of the audience, who will judge a show based on the location of the building in question, as much from the geographical point of view as from the imaginary.

In one of the few pieces of market research carried out into the commercial theatre in Argentina, to assess the pros and cons of staging a US play about AIDS, one participant in one of the focus groups, a professional aged around fifty, recalled how as a student he had generally gone to a lot of independent theatre. Asked if he still went to those theatres, he said no, that 'those theatres are long way away'. I do not think that answer alluded merely to the physical distance between the alternative or fringe theatres and his current home. It is likely that, as time passed, those venues had become 'far away' in the audience member's imagination.

Performance spaces can be analysed, then, from both the *denotative* point of view, in other words based on physical features like the ones mentioned above, and the *connotative*, that is to say based on their ideological traits, the signals that this area, this building, send out into the community where it is located. The way in which a community perceives a particular theatre space shapes the audience's expectations. The ideological image of a space generates a filter through which a show is watched: spaces contain *information* that affects the reception of a play in an imperceptible way. If the actors are not forewarned of this, it can even work against their intentions.

The historical features of spaces

From the creation of Greek theatres, up until the beginning of the twentieth century, theatre production methods established their own spatial forms: the Greek theatre, the Roman theatre, the Elizabethan theatre, the Spanish Golden Age *corral de comedias* (or 'theatre courtyard') and the proscenium arch. In each period, these spaces were always similar. No one could conceive of the different architectural approaches that can be seen today in most cities in the world, where there exist an enormous variety of theatrical spaces.

In times gone by, mises en scène were predetermined by the theatre architecture of each historical period. Plays were written based on the shape not only of the performance area but also of the audience space.

Greek-tragic texts contain all of the elements of the theatre architecture of the period: the *orchestra*, the *skene*, the *paradoi* and *eisodoi* and so on. The same occurs with plays written for Roman theatres: imitations of Greek theatres, with the distinction that while the former allowed nature to be visible behind the performance space, the latter blocked the view with a solid wall decorated with statues of the emperors.

Medieval theatre had no theatre buildings as such, but the traces of the spaces used are inscribed in the texts from the period. From plays for fairs or squares, performed on temporary, portable platforms that allowed for the actors to flee from the authorities who forbade them, to the travelling format of the Passion plays, there is an enormous variety of theatrical possibilities, precisely because of the absence of any particular space. In an era dominated by ecclesiastical rules, theatre could take place in atriums, in monasterial halls or in church porticoes, but also in the great halls of castles for the monarchy or on carts that travelled through poor neighbourhoods. In other words, in locations not specifically designed for theatrical performance.

Elizabethan or Spanish Golden Age texts were first performed on stages erected on the floors of taverns. It was from these constructions that the theatres built later took their particular form: a stage with two levels – or three in some Elizabethan theatres – with a patio or yard depending on the country, which was a space in front of the stage for the audience to stand. Audiences could also watch performances from the balconies lining the internal patios, for an elevated kind of viewing experience.

And finally there are the texts written for the proscenium arch, a space that came to revolutionize theatre architecture because it was the first specific theatre space in an enclosed building, with a framed stage that could hide its inner workings with a new element called a curtain, an object that quickly became emblematic of the theatre. This new device completely transformed not only playwriting – because writers took advantage of the enormous possibilities this kind of stage offered – but also the way in which audiences experienced the theatre phenomenon. Although it is still a very controversial space, continuously debated from both architectural and social perspectives, proscenium arch theatre remains the culmination of all of the previous forms used by the various theatre systems. The appearance of these theatres, invented by the Italians, was a step-change in theatre architecture, because it changed the shape of performance production, and above all of audience expectation, forever.

With the onset of the twentieth century, theatre venues stopped being similar to one another and spaces began to diversify. The hegemony of the proscenium arch, which had replaced Elizabethan theatres or Golden Age courtyards in the seventeenth century, was forced to give way to the use of multiple spaces. Greek and Roman theatres began to be rediscovered, and many of them were repurposed, especially to stage new versions of ancient plays. One example is the Roman Theatre in Mérida, Spain, built between 16 and 15 BCE. Abandoned for a long time, it was first re-used in 1910, and eventually was used to create the Mérida Classical Theatre Festival, and for the premiere of Spanish academic and philosopher Miguel de Unamuno's version of Seneca's *Medea*, opening in 1933 with the renowned Catalan actor Margarita Xirgu in the lead.

But new buildings also appeared that called into question the relationship between play and audience, introducing new ways of arranging the performance space. The best example of this innovation, from 1927, is Walter Gropius and Erwin Piscator's unrealized project, *Totaltheater* (Total Theatre). Its architectural premise is based on the simultaneous coexistence in a single space of a proscenium arch, an arena theatre (or circus) and an amphitheatre, allowing for the use of screens for projections on the walls. All of the theories about 'multi-use spaces', theatre venues that can be modified according to the needs of each show, arose from these ideas from the creator of Bauhaus and one of Germany's most important theatre directors.

The invention of the cinematograph altered performance venues considerably, leading to new spatial arrangements where both art forms coexisted and continue to coexist. In venues known as 'theatre-cinemas', the concept of a proscenium arch (i.e. a stage area with a frame, curtain, flies, wings and 'traps' in the floor of the stage) was retained, but the frontal design of the stages was accentuated, and the boxes on the sides – a legacy of the semicircular forms that had existed earlier, or the horseshoe shape of the *teatro all'italiana* itself – removed.

The circus or arena space also featured among the new venues created for new approaches to the mise en scène. Although it was halfway through the second half of the nineteenth century, the Podestá brothers introduced the circus space for theatre performances to the Buenos Aires scene. In the case of circus itself, a genre was developed that came to be known as *circo con segunda* ('circus with a second half'), because it was made up of circus acts in the first half and a theatre play in the second. Meanwhile, the transition that this company of actors made from circus to theatre came to transform the proscenium arch theatres, turning the orchestra stalls into circus rings. According to comments by some specialists, the mime show *Juan Moreira*, based on the novel by Eduardo Gutiérrez, which premiered at the Podestá-Scotti Circus, was for many the birthplace of 'Argentine theatre' or the 'Argentine national stage'. This idea of the beginning of a national theatre is debatable, but what cannot be denied is the firm establishment of circus as a space for theatre performance.

After the Second World War, the changes continued. As well as using purpose-built theatre venues, the performing arts began using new spaces in buildings originally constructed for other uses. Seamlessly, the performing arts began to inhabit abandoned factories, car mechanics' garages, family homes, basements in blocks of flats and so on. Added to these new places occupied by the performing arts were public spaces like railways stations, public squares, museums or terraces. As if in a new version of the Middle Ages, the Western theatre world filled up with spaces, large and small, which began to be incorporated into the vast array of architectural forms used for the production of theatre.

This diversity of spaces developed at the same time as the new forms that emerged in theatre, dance or musicals. That said, these innovations did not always coincide with a new space. Many of the aesthetic innovations of recent decades took place in the old proscenium arch theatres. Samuel Beckett, to give just one example, revolutionized dramatic language in the middle of the century, but still used all the conveniences of proscenium arch theatre, with its wings, flies and traps.

The shape of the spaces

Unlike what happened until the nineteenth century, however, the absence in our era of architectural models has forced (and continues to force) today's theatre artists constantly to make decisions about the use of the space where the mise en scène takes place.

Although most theatres already have a set way for the play and the audience to interact, because their stages and audience areas are fixed, there are more and more spaces that allow decisions to be made about the location of each and every part of the mise en scène.

Until relatively recently, the mise en scène had to adapt itself to a particular shape, for example a raised stage and stalls. But today a director can decide – as far as the space allows – whether the relationship with the audience will be end-on or in the round, or in any of the variations that invariably arise from these two formats: traverse, semi-circular, thrust, the audience raised up with the play below and so on.

Almost all of the world's state-run theatres have been forced to add alternative spaces to their existing ones. Spaces where the relationship between play and audience can be altered, bringing the audience closer or further away, raising them up or lowering them down, better to appreciate the material being performed. In cases where there is no option of having a new space in a building, other spaces are modified. Sometimes, large stages house both the audience and the play, with the curtain closed and the vast seating area closed off, creating a particular kind of intimacy produced by the incursion of the audience onto a territory that is not usually theirs. In the Teatro San Martín in Buenos Aires, the former cake shop was turned into a theatre space: the Sala Antonio Cunill Cabanellas, a venue with a low ceiling but which allows performances to take various forms. Thanks to this venue's versatility – albeit with its many limitations – the space used for Steven Berkoff's *Decadence* was an area 17 metres long by 4 metres wide, with the audience on both sides. It would have been difficult to achieve this 'corridor' effect in a venue with a stage at one end.

New theatre venues almost always offer the option of transformable spaces. Or at least this is what they intend when they open. Unfortunately, however, habits often develop once they are in use, which tend to leave them fixed in an almost permanent configuration.

The effective space

For any mise en scène to be appreciated at its best, it needs an effective space. One often sees shows in venues that are wrong for them, that work against them or cancel them out. Sometimes this is for purely physical reasons, such as a lack or excess of space in the venue. Shows can feel claustrophobic when they mean to be light and airy, or others get lost in the vastness of enormous theatres. At other times it is for ideological reasons, such as when the space itself has connotations that are obvious or overwhelming. One fairly common example of this phenomenon is when 'anti-establishment' performance pieces take place in state-owned venues with the consent of the authorities, or when plays that contain diatribes against the bourgeoisie are staged in venues where not a single member of that group can be found.

It could be said that the best architectural space for a show would be one created exclusively for one particular mise en scène and never used again. Even though this might seem like nonsense, one of the virtues of great theatre directors is an ability to create the illusion that this space in which the show is taking place is unique and original, did not exist until this moment and will cease to exist once the performance is over. When this does happen, it is thanks to an understanding of all the spatial variables, and of the history of the architectural forms that are always present in any piece of theatre.

The visual arts

The awareness of the eye

Since the beginning of time, theatre has been arranged according to what can be seen. It is a well-known fact that the Greek word *theatron*, which gives the word 'theatre' its origin, means 'place for seeing'. In daily speech, we go to the theatre to *see* a play by such-and-such a person, or we ask someone if they have *seen* the show at such-and-such a theatre. Unless we are referring to a radio programme or a CD audio recording of a play, we do not say 'I'm going to listen to *Hamlet*' or 'Did you hear *The Cherry Orchard* so-and-so directed?' Even though this pre-eminence is only seeming (the visual being just one part of a complex system we call a mise en scène, which requires many other elements in order to exist) it is nevertheless still true that all of the visual images that emanate from a play hold a particular attraction for theatregoers.

Everything seen by the audience when an act of theatre takes place, be it design, set, visual effects, props, costume, make-up or lighting, as well as the shapes of the performers' bodies, belongs invariably to the territory of that discipline that makes objects based on shape, dimension, colour, flats and volumes, levels, lines, light and so on: the visual arts.

The eye is uncompromising in its response to the visual information exhibited on a stage. Many directors often seem not to take this into account. They relegate the visual aspect of a play, failing to realize that not thinking about this amounts to a devastating attack on the chances of attracting an audience. Most potential theatregoers, if faced with an absence of visual ideas, would, to paraphrase Herman Melville's *Bartleby the Scrivener*, prefer not to go.

When a show contains visual elements that do not correspond to a fully-developed visual concept, the eye experiences these as dysfunctional. There are enough examples of this to fill an entire catalogue: threadbare curtains of imprecise, faded hue, trying to pass for a black box; a variety of props such as chairs and mismatched furniture, chosen based on no particular criteria; costumes that are comfortable for the actors but uncomfortable for the eye of the audience; fabrics and designs that do not match the era supposedly being represented; incompatibility between a set specially made for a production and costumes acquired thanks to a deal with some fashion house; painted walls that shake when a door is opened or closed; lighting that shows what should not be seen. Many of these things will inevitably be noticed by those attending the show, leaving the audience with a thankless task that they ought not to have to undertake: using their heads to try to identify what corresponds visually to the material in question and what does not; to work out what is valid and separate it from that which is 'visual pollution', in other words what does not belong within the onstage concept.

For this reason, when all of a show's visual elements are handled artistically, creating a complex component that enriches the mise en scène as a whole, the difference is remarkable. In these shows, the audience is not forced to be distracted from the play.

Despite having designers and other specialists responsible for these visual elements, many shows treat what is seen by the audience as a 'service', as a mere illustration of what is written in the play.

During many periods of theatre history, visual elements had an importance in keeping with the production norms of the day. Although these features were present in theatre's earliest times, the creation of the proscenium arch gave visual matters a major boost that they had never enjoyed before. After a time, perhaps from force of habit, the visual fell into disuse, being used merely to illustrate the requirements of the playtext. But it is with the emergence of the idea of the mise en scène, and of directors as the protagonists of the theatre, that the visual ceased suddenly to occupy such a servile role. Set, costume and lighting designers, all aided by the inclusion of electric light in theatre technology, began to give the visual aspects of the performing arts their autonomy.

Here in Argentina, generations of set and costume designers made work that was fundamental to the development of the visual field. Artists such as Rodolfo Franco, Saulo Benavente and Luis Diego Pedreira, among others, introduced new technologies, helping with their work to alter the way that theatre is seen. And in some state-run or private venues work can still be seen that allows the visual to realize its full potential.

Both in the alternative or fringe theatre and in some productions in state-run or private commercial theatres, however, we are seeing a return to the idea of servitude, relegating visual aspects to the background.

We are in the waters of visual servitude when what the audience sees has no autonomy and is merely a support for what is being narrated. Although the design is of course an active part of the narration of a play, it should be conceived as a visual object that is autonomous of the material that brought it into existence. This is not to say is should be a museum piece: the set, like the props or the costume, are only justified insofar as they relate to the combination of all the materials involved, arranged with an internal coherence that transforms it into a visual object.

To give one example: in play X two characters chat seated at a table in a bar. The first thing to happen will be to pick up the first square table and two chairs one can find and to rehearse with them. Because they have been used in rehearsals, these objects will end up being used for the performance. It is hard for these elements to constitute a visual object in themselves. The most likely thing is that they will betray their origins, which, unless they are processed for the purposes of the play, will create a visual tension that is not always desired. By focussing on the use or usefulness of such objects, we can often fail to see their shape, their texture, their colour, their size and so on. In other words, we fail to see their lack of connection to the artistic.

The visual and its costs

It is often argued that the lack of attention paid to the visual aspects of theatre is caused by the ever-increasing costs of set, costume or, to a lesser extent, lighting design.

In Argentina, outside of the state-run and commercial circuits, where all of those who work on a production receive payment, in most shows that are produced in alternative or independent venues, the work is not paid and the money that can be made is used mainly for sets and costumes.

Lack of money is often used as a justification for not paying attention to the visual approach that any show should have. But it is never advisable for art to care about economic hardship. Quite the contrary: a lack of resources can sometimes mobilize artists and help them discover new forms, adding new visual configurations to the ones that already exist or using new materials hitherto not thought of. Theatre history is full of fine examples of when a lack of funds has given rise to some very powerful aesthetic developments. Caspar Neher's work for Bertolt Brecht, in the impoverished post-war Berlin of the 1920s, is a case in point. Opposing the monumental displays of excess of Max Reinhardt, the spoiled kid of German artistic society, the young Brecht and his designer Neher created a new way of seeing theatre, transforming the stage of the Theater am Schiffbauerdamm, a beautiful theatre in the neo-Baroque style, with the use of throwaway materials like corrugated card, brass, cheap cloth and so forth, unthinkable elements for a theatre production in those times, but which would not have come at great cost to those artists who were almost on the verge of destitution before the enormous success of *The Threepenny Opera* in 1928.

When a show's visual approach lacks rigour, then, the problem lies never with a lack of money, but rather with a lack of regard to the aesthetic needs of the material in question.

And the key to this regard is in the dialogue that should be established, regardless of economic concerns, between the *set, costume and lighting and the visual arts*, where discussions about the difficulties of what is captured by the eye are commonplace, something that the theatre often forgets.

It is very rare nowadays to hear people from the theatre talking about approaches to set design, innovations in costume or major contributions to the field of lighting. Very few artists do it. In general, conversations focus on trying to resolve practical matters, such as pay, rehearsal schedules or interpersonal relationships. Of course, all of these practical problems do need to be solved, but if the visual elements of a show are treated

merely as an obstacle to be overcome, the most likely thing is that
the eyes of the audience will be left wanting.

The eye of the beholder

Any person today, from any social, economic or cultural
background, carries around with them an assortment of highly
developed, elaborate visual data, a product of contact with – and
practical experience of – television, cinema, home-made audio-
visual and photographic recording, the internet and graphics
from both newspapers and magazines and posters on the street.
Potential theatre audiences are filled up with images, some of them
very complex, even though they cannot always decode them clearly
because they rarely possess the technical terminology. Not that they
need to: they are audience members, after all, not specialists.

All of this visual content, carried around by most people who
come into contact with the various image-producing media, is of
considerable modernity. It would be a surprise to be able to list the
whole repertoire of shapes, colours, materials and dimensions that
pass through people's retinae and end up stored in their brains. And
many of these can be classed as art and are extremely elaborate.

It is nothing new to say that contemporary visual art has
always been absorbed by the market for its merchandise and
publicity campaigns. As early as the 1920s, Piet Mondrian shook
the art world with his paintings, with their coloured squares and
rectangles, in search of absolute abstraction. In the early 1930s, the
Polish designer Lola Prusac designed a line of bags and cases for the
house of Hermès, directly inspired by these red, blue, yellow, white
and black artworks.

Artistic images, distributed here and there, hidden in photographs,
in graphic design, printed on fabric, on huge billboards, are
spreading uncontrollably. One need only turn on the television or
the computer, or look at a fashion magazine, to see and be flooded
with shapes that originate in art, even if the use of these images has
no artistic aim.

Theatre – or rather, people who make theatre – tends to forget
about this knowledge, which, albeit unfocused, is very rich and
highly developed. Instead, they abandon the audience. (This does

not happen in the same way amongst people who make dance, much less opera, who tend to be much more attentive to visual knowledge.) And when a play at the theatre does not acknowledge this awareness of the visual, the audience is disappointed. When this happens, audiences begin to compare the poor images offered by the theatre to those displayed at the cinema, on television or on the internet. It is very common to hear most people we know say they prefer the cinema to the theatre. And they are right to, because the theatre very rarely satisfies the desire for the visual.

It is clearly not a matter of theatre trying to rival the visual possibilities of, for example, cinema. This has already been tried and indeed it did surprise for a time. But the truth is it is preferable to watch a real film than to see a play make an enormous effort to seem like a film when it never can be one. Some European directors and their designers attempted this for a while, occasionally wowing their audiences. Some spent a great deal of money, but still they could not solve the problem within theatre itself.

It is simply a case of the visual information that the audience already possesses not being disregarded in the making of a show. Taking it into account, not in order to 'copy' other forms, but in order that the eye of the audience will be attracted by everything that takes place on stage. This way, the enormous frustration, caused by watching shows that do not take into account *the contemporaneity of the eye of the beholder*, would be averted.

Sound art

In every mise en scène there is an approach to *sound* and *time*, the two basic elements of sound art. Throughout its history, this art form has pondered the multiple questions involved in the emission and reception of sound, not only from an artistic point of view, but also with regard to the duration and division of time, and so on, in musical works: in other words, the problem of the physical passing of time in art.

In the performing arts, sound art specifically includes the sounds or noises in a play, music in its stricter sense, the voices of the performers and the question of a show's duration.

How long does something last?

A spectre stalks the theatre: the spectre of boredom. And it appears suddenly, when, during a performance, the audience feels the overwhelming need to know how much time has passed since the beginning and how long it will be until 'it' is over. It is very rare that an audience loses all track of time and ceases to be aware of its passing. This only happens when they are faced with a true work of art, and this experience of losing all sense of time is the height of pleasure. The tremendously uncomfortable feeling of having to stay in a place where one no longer feels like being disappears when what is happening onstage captures the audience completely.

By contrast, the sensation of 'having a body', of being aware of the passing of time, is the most common one in the theatre. There are many factors that cause this feeling, but one of the most powerful is the one that indicates that no thought has been given in the mise en scène to how long the play should last. There are too many shows in which those responsible have not considered the matter of time and, once again, this lack of thought invariably pushes audiences away from theatre venues.

The question of a play's duration is one of the most difficult to answer in the work of direction and demands intense reflection as to the ways in which audiences perceive time.

In the current era, the duration of plays varies. In others, performances had standard running times. I could not tell you how these times were arrived at, because the topic has barely been studied, but the length of the mise en scène of plays in the past can be deduced based on a reading of the texts in their original language and also of reports of the performances and their durations left by some audience members at the time, those who went to the trouble of leaving accounts of such things.

It was in the twentieth century that the matter of stage time began radically to be questioned. Theatrical experiments in which time was stretched to an unbearable extent brought the great theme of time in the mise en scène to the fore. One of the most remarkable shows in this sense was Robert Wilson's *Deafman Glance* (1971), which premiered at seven hours long and consisted of one scene during which one actor crossed the stage diagonally for what seemed like an eternity. Audience members went out into the foyer and came back in later to see if anything had changed. These experiments in prolonged time were catalogued by Hans-Thies Lehmann as the 'theatre of slowness'.

The running time of plays also began to shorten, to the point where some only lasted a few minutes, as we see in some of the texts of Samuel Beckett.

Today's shows, at least most of those that open outside of large-scale theatre venues (which, by the way, are greater and greater in number across the world), tend to last much less time than in the past. It is often thought that this tendency to brevity is happening because the audience is becoming increasingly intolerant of long running times, thanks to the new viewing habits caused by the short times imposed by television and the internet.

But this is not necessarily the case. There are still shows that are long but in which the experience of time remains suspended. In these performances, the pleasure of what the audience sees or hears is not interfered with by the annoyance caused by an awareness of one's own body, which is where the passing of time is truly felt.

Theatre artists often take their own perception of time on stage as being valid for everyone, without taking into account the experience of time as felt by the audience. They even forget their own perception, the one they experience when they watch shows themselves as audience members. They also forget that they are part of a community that has an idea of time, which is perceived in a particular way and which is built collaboratively by all of the community's members. This forgetting drags theatre practice further and further towards a loss of awareness that it *is an art that is produced between the play and the audience.*

And since the theatre act is produced at the intersection between the play (the fiction) and the audience (the non-fiction), it is at this point that the two sensations of time meet and create a new one. This third sensation of time is the mise en scène's true outcome as far as time is concerned, very different from the other two.

A play's running time is directly linked to all of the materials involved in the mise en scène: architecture, visual art, sound and literature. All of these elements work together in a show to contribute to the organization of time. And they do so in relation to 'social time': the notion of time as it is experienced within any given community.

Notions of 'fast', 'slow' and 'just right' are constructs of society and community. These parameters, within which we think of and experience the passing of time, are not uniform or universal. The passing of time is not perceived in the same way in small villages adjoining the countryside as it is in large urban centres.

It is impossible to define how to succeed in finding the exact time, since the art of the mise en scène consists of a *system of relationships* that alter each time any one element changes, for example the variety and difference of the audiences every night. There are shows that can be remarkably different from one performance to the next. The audience can cause a play to last twenty minutes more or twenty minutes less, depending on how much it participates with its laughter or its silences.

When thinking about how long a show should last, it is a case of understanding that a shorter play is not necessarily better, but also that dragging the action out, something that some actors tend to do and that directors allow, does not necessarily mean that a story is unfolding in an interesting way. There are shows that would be excellent if they lasted half an hour, but that extended to an hour and a half become long and tedious. On the other hand, there are shows that should take more time to develop the material presented but that, by not doing so, leave the sensation of something unfinished. There are those that end abruptly, leaving the audience with the feeling that something is missing but without knowing exactly what. And there are shows that go on for so long as to reach crisis point, with the play not caring about the audience at all. Sometimes this results from thoughtlessness or an ignorance of *time*, sometimes it is simply the people responsible wallowing in their own narcissism.

The relationship between time in the play and time for the audience is one of the most complex equations in the art of the mise en scène. I learned this when directing Brecht's *Life of Galileo* at the Teatro San Martín, Buenos Aires, at the end of the 1990s.

The play had previously been staged in the same venue in 1984, shortly after the end of the military dictatorship that devastated our country between 1976 and 1983. The director Jaime Kogan and critic Gerardo Fernández translated the play and wrote the version for the stage. This version placed emphasis on the obscurantism of Galileo's time, something that resonated with the collective experience that we were only just emerging from. The play lasted two and a quarter hours, with no interval. The fervour with which the audience followed the performance meant that the running time was no problem, despite the amount of information contained in the text. At the end of each performance, the auditorium burst into applause, praising not only the performance of the cast led by an extraordinary Walter Santa Ana, but also the possibility of seeing a play by Brecht, a writer banned by the dictatorship.

When fifteen years later I was invited to direct the same play, times had changed. There was no dictatorship any more, so the text could be thought about in a different way. Whilst for Kogan and Fernández the version – beginning with a scene showing the burning of Giordano Bruno, which does not exist in the original play – was an indictment against dictatorships, at the dawn of the new century the play could now recoup some of the original ideas proposed by Brecht, that is to say, the problematic position of intellectuals in relation to power, be that governments, universities, the church or political parties. This also involved a different means of presenting the play, perhaps less fervent, but perhaps, it seemed to me at the time, more analytical. These considerations led me to think that the show needed two intervals, since we were doing the whole play, with no cuts. The two intervals proved to be indispensable for the audience to have their moments of rest from listening to such a long text. The first interval was at the end of Scene Six, when Galileo is accepted in Rome. The second interval was at the end of Scene Ten, which shows how the people, with their carnivals, narrate the events that involve Galileo, in other words the arrival of knowledge to the people. And so it was that this version lasted for three hours and twenty minutes, one hour more than the mise en scène directed by Jaime Kogan.

Nevertheless, despite the show's long running time, there was no sense of exhaustion or stress, and, as in the earlier production, the auditorium was full and erupted at the end into long ovations.

In both versions some thought had been given to the running time, taking into account not only the text, the visual and sound materials and the 1,150-seater auditorium of the Teatro San Martín's Martín Coronado Theatre, but also this mysterious 'concept' of time that audiences have in any given period and which alters from moment to moment.

Music

The presence of music in the performing arts is practically unavoidable. (I refer not to musical theatre or opera, which have music in their structure, nor to dance which, despite its attempts to shed its original dependence on music, still owes it an historical debt.) Although it is not essential, music is generally present in most mises en scène, and in multiple ways. It can appear incidentally, in the guise of an aural commentary on what is happening, or it can be part of the play if music is produced within it in some way: someone listening to music, someone singing a song, or someone playing an instrument as part of the action.

But music has undergone remarkable transformations throughout its history, and so has its inclusion in the theatrical system. It no longer works in the same way as it did in past times.

By linking it to images, audio-visual culture has caused music to lose its autonomy. Aside from specialists (that is to say, composers, instrumentalists, music analysts etc., who are still able to listen to music purely in relation to sound), practically all other people tend to imprint images onto their brains in order to *sustain* their listening. In the twentieth century, first cinema and then television trained the listener-viewer in this listening technique. And although music has no narrative pretensions, listeners will invariably contaminate their hearing with these images, assuming that compositions have a certain amount of narrative content, when in reality they do not.

Theatre tends to make particular use of this *mutation* that music has suffered. It takes advantage of this mechanism that *transforms sound into narration*. In some way, this amounts to a denial of the very idea of musical art. Words (what are the images that arrange themselves in the brain when we listen to music, if they are not words?) are added to this artistic object that has hitherto done without them, being composed instead of pure sound.

I am of course not referring to music that is linked to a text. In these cases, the union between music and literature has a different status to music without words. And even when a composer has given a narrative title to a piece of music, it soon becomes clear that whatever the title says is not contained within the work itself. There is not a single drop of water in Debussy's *La mer*.

Culture, which stabilizes everything that is within its reach (unlike art, which fights always not to be subjugated by culture) has transformed the way we listen to music, and theatre takes advantage of this change, sometimes excessively. It might be said that in most shows music is used not for its intrinsic expressive value as sound, but rather as a scene-setting device or as a locator in time. With the lights turned off, a piece by Gershwin will quickly locate the audience in a city in the United States of America, probably New York. These sounds will for most people evoke this place in the world and possibly a period in time, the 1920s or 1930s, depending on which version is used, just as certain pieces from the Renaissance will signal to us that we are in the court of some sixteenth-century monarch, or a *zamba* in the middle of the Argentine pampa.

It is also used as a 'climate creator', as if musical art were a thermostat that should underpin the audience's emotions. 'Sad' or 'cheery' background music invades plays, causing a clash that often prevents what is being said from being heard. It is thought that adding sound to different parts of the show with a variety of music makes everything more comprehensible. There is no trust that the action itself, the words spoken, the actors' voices or the rhythms used are enough to stimulate the audience's pleasure.

These uses of music are so widespread that even theatre composers themselves often fail to be aware of them. But when one hears Eduard Grieg's *Peer Gynt*, composed for the play of the same name by Henrik Ibsen, one can understand the intrinsic value of music that goes beyond its dependence on the original text and leads the listener along other paths of experience, different from the visual and far removed from narrative.

Today, the huge challenge for composers and arrangers is to create and select music for the theatre that is effective and has some value of its own, so that the music does not play a servile role of mere support, but rather develops in all of its artistic dimensions.

Sounds v. noises

Audiences are used to going to the theatre and hearing many sounds that are not necessarily part of the mise en scène. Most noise pollution occurs in spaces that were not originally intended to be theatres. The techniques of repurposing these venues very rarely take into account the acoustic problem effectively. Voices coming from the street, ambulance, police or fire-engine sirens, the sound systems of passing cars at full volume, televisions shouting from the neighbouring houses or, above all, barking dogs, interfere with the audience without so much as a by-your-leave.

But it is not only in repurposed spaces, which are particularly precarious acoustically, where these invasions take place; they also happen in purpose-built theatres. Our cities grow noisier and noisier and builders have not put in place measures to stop the pounding of the external noise produced by modern life. Today there exist many modern theatre buildings beset by the presence of noises that can be neither controlled nor reduced.

Only the old proscenium arch theatres seem to be protected from such intrusion, since they have in their design some consideration of what is inside (the auditorium) and what is outside (the city); in other words, the necessary soundproofing for protecting the performance. But in the majority of theatre spaces, the necessary barrier for separating the union of play and audience from the outside world is under constant threat from noises that can break through any border.

Those responsible for mises en scène seem not to understand this problem. And yet it is a considerable one, because the audience has to make an extra effort to separate the sounds *from* the show from the noises that break *into* the play, dividing their attention and resulting in a discomfort that causes much of the pleasure promised by the play to be lost.

There are projects that will succeed or fail based on the acoustic conditions of a given space. If the space available does not allow for effective sound design, it is preferable not to attempt them at all.

I will always remember a performance of Tennessee Williams's *The Night of the Iguana* at the Teatro Ateneo, a building in Buenos Aires that had once been a cinema and where no one had thought about the dividing walls with the neighbouring houses. In the middle of a scene that took place in a forest setting, banging began to be heard from an apartment that adjoined the stage. A neighbour was merrily hitting the wall with a hammer in the middle of the night, perhaps unaware that this seemingly private act was ruining a performance that was unfolding in front of many people. The actors tried at first to incorporate the noise, but when they did not succeed (since such banging had nothing to do with the play and its setting), one of the protagonists cast a complicit glance to the audience, which at this point had ceased concentrating on the plot, and cheekily declared, 'It's a neighbour'. We in the audience laughed at this *text* outside of the programme. The banging stopped after a few minutes but the truth was that once the unforeseen interruption of the hammering began it was impossible to restore our attention and a certain unease spread through both the stage and the auditorium.

Acoustic sound or amplified sound

It is increasingly difficult to hear acoustic sound, to perceive sound directly without electronic intervention. Not only does external pollution impede our ability to hear, but the mise en scène also tends not to address adequately the issue of sound, causing too many impediments to the audience enjoying a show.

In both small spaces and large ones with good acoustics, many shows use amplified sound excessively, not only for the playing of music but also to increase the volume of the actors' voices.

One of the problems posed by the indiscriminate amplification of a play – that is, when no complex technical work is involved – is the loss of spatial references. Acoustic sound locates the sources of sound naturally in the space. Without having to think, the audience knows perfectly well where a voice is coming from, how far away those footsteps are, where a particular object has fallen. Amplification, however, alters a sound spatially and disorientates the ear of the audience. Generally, all amplified sounds come from a single source, the speakers located at a certain height, and the different qualities of the sounds onstage are erased.

It is a devilishly difficult thing to create an interesting variety of sounds using amplification. It requires a great deal of work, as well as technology that matches the problems posed. It is not just a matter of making sounds louder, but rather of expressing and interconnecting their individual qualities.

One of the most interesting problems to solve is the combination, in a single show, of amplified and acoustic sound. We know that each of these appeals to a different part of the brain in order to be heard. For this reason, the coexistence of both forms in one play can make it harder for an audience to hear. Switching from one to the other will always cause serious problems if no thought is given as to how to articulate these transitions. (That is, unless one wants to cause an aural disaster in the audience, which happens to be a very interesting expressive technique: because we hear decibels differently in acoustic versus amplified form, the jump between acoustic and amplified sound causes a kind of temporary deafness.)

Some time ago, in a very large Buenos Aires theatre with good acoustics, I saw a show that began with a song, performed by an opera singer who, in addition to his own vocal projection, used a microphone accompanied by a recorded backing track played over the speakers located beyond the stage. This opening number lasted for about five minutes. No sooner had he finished his song than some actors entered the stage speaking acoustically. For several minutes the words they were saying were impossible to understand. The brains of those of us present were trying to change the way we were listening. During the time it took for the ear to do this work, it was impossible to hear the words they were saying because they seemed *muffled*, distant. Neither the director nor the musical director of this work seemed at any point to be aware of this, because the same device was used throughout the play without interruptions, switching from one system of sound to the other. That said, although it may cause the same problems for hearing, the switch from acoustic to amplified sound is less 'traumatic' to the ear.

I want to stress that it is not a case of using the same system throughout (the two available forms can of course be mixed), but rather of considering how this mixture can best be applied, how each system appeals to a method of listening and which of these would have the best expressive result.

Another problem that occurs, especially with amplified sound, is the relationship with real space. Most people can establish a link between the sound they hear and the space containing this sound. Acoustic sound accounts for this relationship perfectly, while amplified sound can alter a space's boundaries. A 100-piece symphony orchestra would be impossible to listen to in a small venue. The sounds would intermingle, denying the ear the pleasure it might have in listening; instead of music, there would be an unbearable racket. On the other hand, an acoustic piano in a football stadium would be inaudible were it not for amplification to cover this immense space. The tensions and strains between sound and space are an expressive element that flows through any mise en scène, and although there are no hard and fast rules about these relationships, one should not fail to think about them.

Voices

Although actors have highly developed physical abilities, the voice is still the indicator of the quality of their performances (except, obviously, in the case of mimes or those who work in what is known as the 'theatre of the image', because their art is founded on the visual).

Unlike opera singers, who can possess very musical voices even if this talent may not guarantee a good stage performance, in spoken theatre it is generally the actors' voices that shape the audience's enjoyment.

Actors are, among other things, producers of sound and, like instrumentalists with no score, when they say words, be they their own or someone else's, have to select and combine musical parameters. The interconnection of the literary text with the sound of the voice, that is to say the *mise en son* of literary material, is truly one of the greatest challenges facing an actor during rehearsals, since they must find the appropriate sounds for this text in their voices.

It might be said that good actors are those who know how to arrange sounds effectively in accordance with the words that they say, a quality one does not always find. They know from experience, even if they have never put it into words, that when one thinks about the expressive aspect of acting, one must also have a care for the sound quality of the voice, working with the parameters of volume, intensity and speed, all in relation to one's own timbre, that sound characteristic that makes every person different to the other. In other words, with all the elements that make the production of sound more or less effective.

As an audience member one often experiences a disconnect between the text and the sound of the voice. We have all at some point heard 'heroic' actors, with intense voices and perfect diction, struggling with realist, naturalist or genre texts, giving them unnecessary transcendence when the authorial intention was to reproduce day-to-day speech without the need for any kind of emphasis. But many other times we have seen the efforts of some actors who end up mistreating very elaborate texts, like those of Greek tragedy or by contemporary authors with strong narrative content, who fail in their performance because they lack the technical and expressive resources to be able to perform them. It is surprising how little importance is given to these matters in mises en scène.

But it is not simply a case of the relationship between the voice of the actor and their lines, but rather of the interconnection between all of the actors' voices and the material used for the show. The more voices there are, the greater the stress placed on sound. When there is only one voice, the audience tends not to have problems, because they do not need to make a decision. This is because there is only one voice signalling to the listener which path they should take. But when there is more than one voice and the mise en scène has not developed an approach to how the sounds of the voices should be treated, listening becomes more difficult.

It is common to see a show and hear how the actors in the play do not produce sound in the same way. This is not the same as the linguistic tics used in genre plays to distinguish between the voices of different characters; ultimately, these are literary devices used to try to imitate certain kinds of spoken language. I refer rather to those mises en scène where the actors themselves have different ways of generating sound. Perhaps the popular Argentine expression that best describes this situation might be 'de cada pago, un paisano':[5] in any one place, there are always people from many different places.

The diversity of acting schools, combined with the various trends in voice work – something that began to appear halfway through the twentieth century – has led to actors appearing on one stage with very different ways of making sound. If this is not worked on consciously and expressively, it can cause serious problems for the audience trying to hear. Two actors who each make sound in a different way (someone might simply call this different ways of acting) force the audience to pick one of them as the effective one, leaving the other one seeming defective.

Let us imagine a great actor, very famous, one of those whom the audience loves and with whom they identify immediately, who possesses a very powerful vocal instrument, acting in a realist play, accompanied by a cast trained in an acting technique that produces a remarkable effect of 'naturalness'. The most likely thing is that the general public – which is the true audience – would be bewildered, and might choose their favourite actor as the lead performer to listen to, the one that the culture has imposed as 'the best actor'. And even if this actor in artistic terms might be defective in this show, with the other actors being the ones on the correct road, the audience will struggle throughout the whole play, trying to understand 'how' they should listen, tugged at by their choice. With their voices, with their sounds, actors good and bad impose a mode of listening onto the audience. When there are various different ways of making sound onstage, the audience is forced to choose one of them in order to break the tension generated in them by hearing forms of sound that are so different as to be impossible to blend together.

---

[5]Roughly translated, 'one countryman from every parish'. A *pago* refers to a region, district or estate; a *paisano* can mean a peasant, or a fellow citizen. (Translator's note.)

How can these differences be recognized? In the way in which the voices are located in the actors' vocal apparatus, in how the sound of the voice is projected, in how the words are pronounced, in how the sounds are 'attacked', in the way in which the qualities of the sound are worked on and so on. In other words, all of the problems they may cause for the construction of an overall vocal sound design.

It is a case then of tending towards the *harmonization* of sound so that the audience can concentrate its attention on the artistic and not on the badly handled technical aspects of the play. When the audience is forced to make a choice, this makes listening uncomfortable and can lead the audience to fall into a state of distraction.

Mises en scène produced by permanent companies, or by groups that have worked together for a long time, or by casts made up of actors who all have the same acting technique – in other words, by any group of performers who have in some way been connected for a long time – usually allow for an ease of listening that is quickly picked up on by the audience. In all of these cases, there usually exists, regardless of artistic quality, a balance of sound resulting from the cast having spent so much time together.

Sometimes, time spent working together in a group causes actors to develop a common way of producing sound that even they are completely unaware of. Because of this, in shows produced with casts assembled specifically for one particular production, it is most likely that the interconnection of sound necessary for the audience to enjoy the show will not be achieved. And this is the case regardless of the particular qualities of each actor. This problem occurred in a production of *Los Reyes de la Risa* (*The Kings of Laughter*), a version of Neil Simon's *The Sunshine Boys* staged a few years ago in Buenos Aires, with Alfredo Alcón and Guillermo Francella. Everyone knew who was who: Alcón, a huge actor with a long history in theatre, especially playing heroic roles, and Francella, a well-known and extremely funny comic actor, especially on television. Each of them very effective on his own. The presence of both actors on stage was a first and attracted big audiences. But this did not prevent the audience from having the thankless task of having to choose one actor or the other, because, from the point of view of sound, they were not in the same show. The producers of this play probably did not care too much about addressing the issue of the differing approaches to the voice, given the box-office success that this pairing produced. But, on the way out of the theatre, at the end of the performance, it was common to hear the phrase, 'You don't know which one to choose', said as if it were a compliment, when in fact it was an incredible description of what the audience perceived but could not express with the adequate words, something that tends to happen very often to those who go to the theatre.

Literature

The words

There is no need to take up much space elaborating ideas about literature. Since time immemorial, people have thought and written about the words that tell stories, express feelings, describe events. In any of its forms, be it chronicles, short stories, novels, poems, plays, essays and the rest, literature has always been and remains today a constant source of material for the scholars of words. In the specifically theatrical field, the first such scholar was Aristotle, who dedicated his *Poetics* to tragedy and its rules. Since then, dramatic literature has stood for a long time at the centre of any discussion about theatre, most likely because the written text is one of the most stable 'leftovers' of theatre activity. While theatre spaces disappeared, actors died and costumes corroded in badly ventilated trunks, texts remained unaltered, regardless of technological changes in the formats they were preserved in. From the wax tablet to the book, dramatic texts survived the passing of time unchanged, allowing those who defended the pre-eminence of the literary character of the dramatic text over a performance to have arguments that were considered indestructible.

The often brutal hand of the designer or director immobilizes the very things that had a moving, fleeting grace, turning what was only a game for our imagination into a kind of trompe-l'oeil. In the middle of a painted cardboard country scene, under unrealistic lighting, imperfections of all kinds accumulate, imperfections in set, in costume, in movement, in gesture, in diction, which are as much an affront to poetic beauty. These are indeed the disastrous conditions under which a play appears at the theatre.

So stated the French man of letters Louis Becq de Fouquières in *The Art of the Mise en Scène* in Paris in 1884.[6]

But it is in the late nineteenth century, with the emergence of the specific work of the director in the theatre system, that this hegemonic place that dramatic texts have held starts to be reduced and the mise en scène begins to be thought of as something very different to the mere mechanical transfer of the literary text to the stage.

For a long time now, it has not been necessary to have a pre-existing dramatic text to be able to put on a show. Literary material can be created in rehearsals and it is likely that the final version of the text performed on the stage will only emerge shortly before the show's opening night.

But whatever the method of work, literature is inescapably present in the mise en scène as one of its four constituent art forms. It is present in the playtexts that have already been written in the past or the present, in the actors' improvisations, in the linking together of the actions of narrative sequences; it is there wherever there are words that aim to be artistic, whatever form they may acquire in the context of a work of art.

From poetic language to the most coarse, the words that flow through a theatre production, in dance-theatre, in musical theatre, in opera, will always have a literary connection. Playwriting, ultimately, is but one category of literature.

But the realm of words is not limited to those that are arranged as text in the show. It can also be said that in every mise en scène there exists an interconnection between the words that are said during the play and the ones that are produced during the working process, those that are spoken during rehearsals that come to constitute the scenic act. In the field of art, we know that the use of words does not follow the rules of day-to-day speech, and as such any words that are used during the putting-on of a show (work codes, forms of evaluation made every day, daily anecdotes told during free time, gossip etc.) become part of the literary baggage that is ultimately interwoven into the mise en scène. It is not a case of talking in an artificial way during the rehearsal process, but rather of being aware that the way in which anyone

---

[6]Becq de Fouquières, Louis, *L'Art de la mise en scène* (Paris: G. Charpentier et Cie, 1884), pp. 10–11. Translation for this volume by William Gregory.

expresses themselves in relation to the material being worked on develops, given that it is an artistic process, a form of literature.

In my personal experience I have noticed that various materials or texts 'force' one to express oneself orally during rehearsals in a particular way in order to be in tune with the texts (or planned texts) one is working with. The way in which the material is worked on in order to express it in the mise en scène is in some way led by the uncovering of its literary characteristics. I am not talking just about its plot, if it has one, but of its poetics, its particular use of language. In other words, everything that literature and its scholars have been exploring for a long time.

Language

In the field of literature, we have no problem talking about language, because here we have *words* and *structures*. But one should not use the word 'language' when applied to space, sound or the visual. In artistic and academic circles, concepts such as 'sound language', 'visual language' or 'the language of space' are harped on about ad nauseam, and it is almost impossible to eradicate this habit imposed by some currents of extra-artistic thought that seem to afford the word 'language' more prestige than the word 'art'. But I have no desire to go into this overly long and boring discussion, which takes place outside of theatre practice in arenas that attempt to study the performing arts based on categories that are not always necessary for understanding art, and much less for producing it.

In the case of non-literary art forms, those made up of shapes, colours, sizes, sounds, the timbre of instruments and so on, we may use words to explain them, but their materiality cannot be reduced to words. They are perceived through the senses, through their presence, and not, as is the case in language, through the absence of the object. If a stage direction in a text says, 'She wears a red dress that rustles as she walks', the reader may well imagine what 'she' is like, the shape of that dress, the particular shade of this red and the sound of the rustling. But none of this will be the same as seeing and hearing this dress in motion. And in the theatre we are always seeing and hearing concrete things, rather than words describing absent objects.

One of the most intense challenges for a mise en scène is directly connected to this particular characteristic of literature, which expresses itself in words and through the absence of the 'thing' being named or referred to, and the multiple effects produced by its coexistence onstage with the arts of perception – the visual, the spatial and sound. As any linguist will tell you, words describe that which is absent. Spoken or read, their effectiveness is always linked to there being a lesser amount of visual or sound information present when we read them. We have all gone through the thankless experience of seeing a novel we have enjoyed reading adapted for the cinema. We are disappointed by practically all of it: the appearance and voices of the characters, the locations where the action takes place, the editing so different to the pace with which we read the book. Nothing of what we read matches what we are seeing and hearing.

For that reason, one of the great problems of dramatic literature is precisely its interconnection with the other art forms. Perhaps this is the reason why for centuries the study of theatre was the study of the text itself, and not of the performed play. The text is, for those scholars of the past, imaginable outside of physical performance, something that according to some devalues the text itself, to the extent of calling what happens onstage a 'beggarly art that needs others'.[7] Luckily, today, things can be thought of differently and dramatic literature can be put in its rightful place.

The hypothesis of performance

A common question often asked inside and outwith the theatrical arena is this: 'What defines whether a text is theatrical or not?' There is no single answer to this question, but certainly a text is not theatrical just because it is written as a dialogue (or as a monologue). The usual form of playwriting, one that indicates the names of the characters, that describes the place where the action occurs or which refers to sounds – in other words, that contains what is known as *stage directions* – does not guarantee that a text is meant for the stage. If this were all that were necessary, we

---

[7]Barbey d'Aurevilly, Jules, *Le Théâtre Contemporain* (Paris: PV Stock, 1908), p. 9. Translation for this volume by William Gregory.

would have to include non-theatre texts such as Plato's *Dialogues* or Galileo's *Discourses*, or some chapters of James Joyce's *Ulysses*.

By contrast, Heiner Müller's *Hamlet Machine*, which is not written as dialogue, and in which there is no indication of characters, or of set, and so on, is a playtext, or at least it has come to be used in this way as the raw material for numerous mises en scène, starting from the moment it was written.

So what in a text identifies it as strictly speaking theatrical? The presence of characters or a strong conflict are not what defines the theatrical. These same elements can be found in novels, in short stories or in poems. Even a police report has more dramatic elements than one might suppose, without it being a theatre play. What defines the presence of the theatrical in a text is the *hypothesis of performance*: a pre-empting of the scenic act in its physical form, as revealed through the markers present in the text itself that refer directly or indirectly to the systems of theatrical production particular to the moment when the texts were written.

The multiple elements of a dramatic text, such as, among other things, the arrangement of time (acts, scenes etc.), the number of characters present in each scene, the approach to space or the types of language in its stricter sense, are predetermined by the conditions of theatre production of each period.

To give some examples: in Greek tragedy we can see how the organization of scenes and the relationships between characters are determined by the number of actors set by the theatrical system of the time. We know that in all tragedies the distribution of the roles of the various characters was thought out to allow for a performance by a very small number of male actors (two in the tragedies of Aeschylus or three in those of Sophocles and Euripides) who, thanks to the use of masks, could switch from one character to another, male or female, sometimes with enormous difficulties in the changes. If we read them carefully, despite having many more than three characters, not all of the characters are onstage at the same time. Some of the actors have to exit the scene in order for another character to be able to enter, of course wearing a different mask.

In *Hippolytus* by Euripides, the character of Phaedra, who kills herself inside the palace, is brought in on a bed, placed atop the *ekkyklema*, a rolling platform brought in by servants. The actor who in earlier scenes played the poor wife who falls in love with her stepson is not the one lying now in the nuptial bed: he now appears hidden behind the mask of Theseus who, along with the actors playing Hippolytus and the Nurse, takes part in the next episode. The mask of Phaedra is now worn by an 'extra' who remains lying down in the bed.

At other times, characters appear mute in the scene, not uttering a single word from their entrance to their exit. This is the case of Ismene, in Sophocles' *Oedipus at Colonus*. In one of the final scenes, she appears with Oedipus, Antigone and Theseus, but does not open her mouth. Clearly, whoever played that part was not one of the three actors, but a stand-in or extra.

This category also included small children, such as Medea's children, or servants, such as Clytemnestra's in *Agamemnon*, because these did not fall into the categories of protagonist, antagonist or tritagonist, the only ones that moved the action forwards. In the same way, the coryphe, the representative of the chorus in the play, was not included in the category of actor either.

The possible combinations of entrances and exits by the actors was what determined, ultimately, the construction of the episodes of all of the Greek tragedies.

In the texts of Elizabethan theatre, defined by the characteristics of the spaces of the period, the characters who participate in a play never remain onstage at the end: almost always, at the end of a scene, one of the characters says 'Let's away!' or 'Let's within!' People are always coming in and going out of scenes and it is unlikely, or rather impossible, for a character who is present at the end of a scene to be the same one who begins the next. With one exception: in Act Four, Scene Five of Shakespeare's *Henry IV, Part 2*, King Henry asks to be taken to another room. At the beginning of Scene Five, the same king is in the scene, already in bed. This scene is so exceptional in Elizabethan writing, a playwriting form so dependent on the shape of its spaces, that in some critical editions, commentators take the trouble of explaining this movement in which King Henry is taken from one room to another, or rather from one scene to the next.

In the writing of these texts, even the amount of time it would take for the actors to get from one spot to another, or to change costumes, was taken into account. Speeches that seem pointless can therefore be understood: they exist to buy the actors time.

Shakespeare constructed all his texts with absolute regard to the arrangement of space in the different theatres where his plays opened. But there are also markers of the physical characteristics of the actors who originated certain roles in his texts: in *A Midsummer Night's Dream*, mention is made of Hermia's small stature in relation to Helena, a reference that is also present in *As You Like It* between Rosalind and her cousin Celia. It is likely that the actors in the company who originated these female roles had this physical difference, something that preceded the writing of these plays and was considered and included by the author. The number of characters in the plays is also a marker of the time when they were each produced, because they are more numerous when the company had more stability and there are fewer actors when conditions were not such that performances could be guaranteed. During the plague from 1592 to 1594 Shakespeare only wrote two comedies, with very few characters in comparison with his other plays.

Texts written and premiered since the creation of the proscenium arch theatre, with its new technologies, changed playwriting again. This fact can clearly be seen in the use of *stage directions*. From the Greeks to the Elizabethans or the Spanish Golden Age, all indications of location were included in the characters' lines. Thanks to them, the audience could know if the action was taking place outside a temple or a palace, in the middle of a forest or in a royal chamber. But when the theatre spaces changed, *stage directions* began to be written independently of the text spoken by the characters and it became possible to indicate where the scenes were happening without any need for the locations to be spoken by the characters, because the set design would supply the necessary information. The theatrical machinery of the proscenium arch theatre made possible many *narrative devices* that earlier architectural forms had not been able to develop. One of the most remarkable of these was the use of the curtain, which allowed a play to begin without any visual information being given away beforehand, as well as being able to hide the scene changes. For a long time, playwrights ended acts with the word 'curtain'. Some of them gave this an expressive character such as 'slow curtain' or 'fast curtain', and so on. By the twentieth century, we can read several alternatives for the end of an act or a play. To the ones already mentioned are added 'blackout', 'darkness' or nothing at all.

With a few exceptions, most of the playtexts written today, be they by single authors or groups working together, are conceived for few actors and with practically no scene changes. Just as no one would think of composing an opera unless commissioned to do so by some organization guaranteeing to premiere it, playwrights do not think of writing plays that envisage hugely elaborate stagings.

It is not possible yet to look at these plays historically, but it is quite likely that many years from now, those researching the playwriting of today will be able to study the patterns of writing – the hypotheses of performance – which, consciously or not, steered writers in the literary production of their texts: small spaces, lack of sufficient technology to allow for scene changes, plays with few characters, an abundance of monologues, unpaid casts and so on. Factors that are all present within their texts.

When directing a play based on a text from the past, even from the recent past, it is necessary to seek out the markers of the systems of theatre production inscribed within it. These are the key to understanding the deep structure of the material and to deciphering its codes, which can sometimes seem mysterious. When working with a dramatic text, some theatre artists reject the notion of a *hypothesis of performance* contained within it, believing it will restrict the *creativity* of the artists. But the opposite is true: not taking this hypothesis into account will likely lead to more mistakes being made than are tolerable. For as Barthes said, 'The better we know the history of the theatre, the more power we will have over its future.'[8]

Texts to be read or texts to be heard

All texts spoken on stage should be understood immediately. The theatre audience does not have the option that a reader of a book has of looking back up the page to reread something they have not understood. Furthermore, the audience, unlike the reader, cannot impose the pace at which the text is being delivered, while the reader can, by adjusting the speed with which they read as they choose.

Audiences tend to get stuck on expressions or phrases that they have not managed to understand, and this diverts their attention from the words that follow. This is not always the fault of the actors,

---

[8]Barthes, Roland, *Écrits sur le théâtre*, ed. Jean-Loup Rivière (Paris: Éditions du Seuil, 2002), p. 182. Translation for this volume by William Gregory.

who should be able to transmit their lines with the greatest possible clarity. It is sometimes a problem of literary construction, where it is obvious that there has been no consideration of the intelligibility of the words being emitted.

It is in translations where these issues are most often present, because here the original language – with its particular sounds or syntax, which gives the whole thing coherence regardless of the complexity with which a text is written – is not being used.

In its original language a text has an internal logic that sustains it, but when translated this quality can disappear. Good translations are those that allow the original content to be understood, and that find a linguistic coherence in the language into which they are being translated that is equivalent to – but never the same as – that of the original text.

But in the Spanish-speaking world this is not common in the theatre, which tends to work with translations carried out according to the same literary (i.e. non-theatrical) criteria used for short stories or novels, which are largely unrelated to what the theatre needs in order for the audience to understand the text clearly and above all quickly.

In a text intended exclusively for reading, the malfunctions of translation are generally tolerated a little more because the average reader pays much more attention to the events of the narrative than to the form of the writing. The Spanish-speaking Latin American reader often puts up with translations from Spain that are completely alien to them. But when a translation from Argentina is used in Spain or elsewhere in Latin America, the Argentine word for 'you' – 'vos'[9] – has to be used, even though it is practically incomprehensible outside of Argentina or Uruguay.

---

[9]Translator's note: Spanish has a number of ways to say 'you'. 'Tú' is the familiar, singular form, used universally across all Spanish-speaking countries. 'Usted' is the formal, singular form. In some countries including Argentina, there also exists 'vos'. Although understood in other Spanish-speaking countries, it is not in general use worldwide. The challenge when translating is further complicated by the different conjugations of verbs depending on which word for 'you' is used. To take the example of *llorar* ('to cry'): 'you cry' would be translated as 'tú lloras' (with the stress on 'llor'), 'usted llora' (the same stress), or as 'vos llorás' (with the stress on 'rás'). These different conjugations not only sound different in terms of national dialect, but if changed can alter the rhythm of the dialogue because of where the stressed syllables lie.

This use of the pronoun 'vos' is exclusive to the River Plate area, and causes problems when used in translations of classic plays when they are staged. Some plays – Chekhov's, for example – are robust enough to withstand the use of 'vos' with no great difficulty. But something very strange emerges when the actors have to perform classical texts that are not – unlike those of Lope de Vega or Lorca – originally written in Spanish. The question always arises: whether to use the Argentine-Uruguayan 'vos' form, or the more universal 'tú'. As a result, one often sees mises en scène where the actors switch between 'vos' and 'tú' without the slightest logic, making the language jar. Ingrid Pelicori, who in addition to being an excellent actor is also an exquisite translator, to avoid the use of different conjugations that come from the indiscriminate use of 'tú' and 'vos', created a system to avoid their use entirely. It is a very complex, but possible technique. She used it for a production I directed of *The Trojan Women*, and for a version of *Hamlet* directed by Manuel Iedbadni. On another occasion, Lautaro Vilo and I used the same device in the translations and versions of *King Lear* and in *Henry IV, Part* 2.

Here is one example of many. Cassandra says to her mother in a line from Euripedes-Sartre:

Prends le flambeau, mère,
mène le cortège.
Qu'est-ce qu'il y a? Qui pleures-tu?

[Take the torch, mother,
lead the cortège.
What's the matter? For whom do you cry?]

This phrase could be translated into Spanish using the imperative voice (giving direct instructions: '*take* the torch; *lead* the cortège') and the 'tú' form, as follows:

Toma la antorcha, madre,
dirige el cortejo
¿Qué pasa? ¿A quién lloras?

Or using the 'vos' form, thus:

Tomá la antorcha, madre,
dirigí el cortejo
¿Qué pasa? ¿A quién llorás?

(Note the difference in stress between *Toma* and *Tomá*, *dirige* and *dirigí*, *lloras* and *llorás*.)
Pelicori's version reads:

Madre, te pido que tomes la antorcha,
y dirijas el cortejo.
¿Qué pasa? ¿A quién estás llorando?

The use of 'te pido que' ('I ask you to') avoids the conjugation of the imperative, without losing the function of a command. The use of the gerund '¿A quién estás llorando?' ('For whom are you crying' as opposed to 'For whom do you cry') does the same with the question. With incredible subtlety, Pelicori avoids giving the language a rancid flavour, in which the 'translation' as such can be heard.

A theatre text always has to have a relationship with spoken language without losing contact with literature. A text can transmit very complex ideas, but demands a high-quality poetic construction, in accordance with the ideas that it intends to express, so that it can be listened to and understood sensitively. And above all, the language must flow imperceptibly so that the audience does not find itself caught in nets of words it does not understand. Being trapped like this interrupts the pleasure the audience has come to the theatre to seek. Texts badly written in their original language or bad translations of great works only push audiences away from theatre venues.

One of the authors worst treated by translations is Shakespeare. Publications of his plays demonstrate the contemptuous lack of thought that translators (and their editors) have given to the need for these texts not only to be read but also to be listened to. In Hispanic America we have had to suffer the translations of the Spanish writer and translator Luis Astrana Marín, who – *noblesse oblige* – made a colossal effort to translate the English bard's complete works into Spanish for the first time and whose resulting work became the basis for many mises en scène. But his work is filled with phrases that are impossible to understand, with complicated constructions that attempt to convert Elizabethan English into an anachronistic Golden-Age Spanish, filled with words that were unknown even at the time of translation (1929), and so forth. A good example is the famous monologue, 'To be or not to be', from *Hamlet*, where he translates the simple expression 'sea of troubles' as 'piélago de calamidades' ('a deep ocean of calamities'). Surely, a florid use of words worthy of the great Baroque poet Luis de Góngora himself.

The majority of Spanish-speaking actors studied Shakespeare's plays using these translations, not noticing that it is impossible to act with them effectively. The excessively complex syntax, the needlessly convoluted lexis, the lack of dynamism in the construction of the lines, are always plain to see in the bodies of the actors and cause tension when they reach the audience.

It is often thought that there are some texts that are very difficult to understand on a first hearing, and this is true up to a point. To give immediate pleasure, a text by Calderón de la Barca not only needs the right actors to handle the language of the Golden Age, able to project such complex lines, but also audiences trained in verse and in the language of the seventeenth century. But it is worth pointing out as an aside that good theatre does not need the audience to have had any previous training: good works of art capture them regardless of whatever knowledge they may have.

It was during the performances of Calderón de la Barca's *Casa con dos puertas mala es de guardar* (*A House with Two Doors is Hard to Guard*), which was included in a show that took place on two stages entitled *The Golden Age of Peronism* (the other stage had *Comunidad organizada* [*Organized Community*], which I co-wrote with Marcelo Bertuccio) that I realized the effect of complex texts on audiences. For about the first ten minutes, no one understood very much, but after this period of time their ear grew accustomed to this style of language so far-removed from the present. And from that moment on, and despite their not understanding every single word (especially those complex expressions and terms that have fallen out of use and are very difficult to understand on a first hearing), the audience began to enjoy the show, following the events, the plot twists and above all the humour of the play. It was remarkable how they switched from not understanding to understanding: after a few anxious minutes thinking they would not understand a thing, the audience began to relax. In this kind of text, the audience's ear is similar to that of someone listening to music: what it does not understand through meaning is captured by the *shape* of the text.

Actors, directors and playwrights seem not to be very well informed of how little is known about the language that should be used for acting, directing or writing. At least in Argentina, studying the Spanish language is not obligatory for theatre training, in either private or state-owned institutions. At Argentina's Universidad Nacional de las Artes (National University of the Arts), neither the BA courses in Acting or Directing nor the MA in Playwriting have any trace of any teaching about issues of language for students of these different branches of theatre. Nor does the Playwriting course at the Escuela Metropolitana de Arte Dramático (Metropolitan School of Dramatic Art). In Mexico, on the other hand, Spanish is a compulsory module in actor training at the Centro Universitario de Teatro (University Theatre Centre) at the Universidad Nacional Autónoma de México (National Autonomous University of Mexico).

This ignorance of language causes serious problems for the staging of shows, especially those using texts by contemporary authors such as Jean-Luc Lagarce, Bernard Marie Koltès, Heiner Müller, Marcelo Bertuccio, Alejandro Tantanian, Lautaro Vilo and Luis Cano, among others, because their texts demand an enormous amount of work from actors and directors on language.

None of these playwrights can be tackled with limited knowledge of the language they are being performed in. It is because of a systematic lack of knowledge of language that mises en scène of these plays are often defective. Boredom replaces pleasure when listening to them, and this means, once again, that the audience will – metaphorically and/or literally – run away.

Text analysis

Ever since universities became part of the theatre education system, generally via so-called (oddly) 'combined' arts degrees, some new problems have appeared in the theatre. One of these relates to the analysis of texts. Probably all degree courses in which theatre is studied have a module dedicated to the analysis of playtexts. But although the methods used in these modules may be very useful for non-dramatic texts, they are of very little use for the range of plays that have been written from the Greeks to the present day.

Literary theory is a discipline that certainly merits study, but whether one knows much about literary theory or not, one should not doggedly apply the same models of analysis to different texts. When trying to understand different materials, using the same methodology for all of them is unlikely to lead to the right destination. It is a process contrary to artistic thought and doubtless more appropriate to academic needs than to artistic ones. Each text requires a distinct method of artistic analysis, a different approach. The model of opposing forces can be used on a play by Shakespeare, but it is practically useless for Samuel Beckett's *Not I*. And it has been known for some poor students to make a real hash of their acting by trying to apply the Greimas actantial model to every text placed before them.

Academics today often resemble a copy of Charlie Chaplin in one of his short films. If memory serves, I recall Chaplin playing a drunken aristocrat. He receives a letter in which his lover tells him she is leaving him, so he turns his back to the camera and cries. He appears to be shaking with inconsolable weeping, but when he turns around we see he is shaking a cocktail shaker. Then he decides to pack his bags. He throws his belongings into the suitcase willy-nilly, and closes it. As some of his clothes poke out from the edges, hanging outside the case, he cuts off the excess cloth with some scissors. And thus he takes the suitcase. I think some 'scholars' do the same thing as Chaplin: they pack the case, destroying the clothes. They analyse the text, making cuts here and there, however it suits the model of analysis, instead of allowing the textual material itself to make it clear how it should be read (and as a result how it should then be worked on for the mise en scène). Each author, and each play within that author's oeuvre, contains very different elements that cannot be treated as though they were all the same.

Another mistake that is made in academia is letting oneself be led by the reputation that playwrights are given, the label that comes attached to them when they are studied. I refer to 'the doxy of the author', the opinion that the culture has built around playwrights and that transforms, for example, Lorca's *Blood Wedding* into a conventional rural play, when in reality it is a work of enormous complexity that moves from lyricism to the most extreme surrealism in its description of settings, as well as the use of different forms of writing: prose, free verse, octosyllables. Many people are often surprised when they read the stage directions. For example in the final scene:

> *White room with arches and thick walls. Right and left, white staircases. Large arch upstage and wall of the same colour. The floor will also be gleaming white. This simple room will have the monumental sense of a church. There will be no grey and no shadow, not even enough for perspective.*[10]

It is the play itself that should steer the analysis. This is a much more difficult task, because one cannot rely on a single method, but it allows multiple ways of approaching the text to emerge, from different sources and from different currents of thought.

So when analysing a text for performance it is viable to leave an empty space and to try instead to work out what the text itself is suggesting. We can break with the idea that we have to do something *to* the text. It is much more interesting, theatrically speaking, for the text to do something to us. Theatrically speaking.

---

[10]García Lorca, Federico, *Bodas de sangre* (Madrid: Cátedra, 1994), p. 155. Translated for this volume by William Gregory.

PART TWO

The director's place

One of the greatest difficulties in understanding the precise place of the director is perhaps their relative novelty in the history of Western theatre. Although since its origins in Greek theatre there has always been someone responsible for what happened onstage, the figure of the *director* as part of the theatrical system did not exist in the way we know it today until the mid-nineteenth century. In various eras, it was poets, actors, designers or stage managers who arranged the elements of the play according to existing performance models. Although Aeschylus, a playwright, actor and stage manager, introduced the second actor into Greek tragedy (according to what Aristotle wrote in his *Poetics*), he made no substantive alterations to overall methods of staging. The same thing occurred with Shakespeare and his contemporaries, who worked according to the model of production of Elizabethan theatres. In the main, playwrights had to adapt themselves to rules previously set by the modes of production that predetermined the writing. At least in the case of antiquity, we do not know who it was that set these methods of production, but the likelihood is that they were established by practice itself, in other words by the shows themselves being staged in succession.

The texts that arose from these previous models already had all of the arrangements for the production of the play written into them, a sort of guide to the staging of the text, which could be followed by the writer themselves, a lead actor, a designer or an impresario. There was no concept of creativity in what was staged, and of course no one complained about this.

According to the historian Edward Braun in his *The Director and the Stage*, it was more recently, in the second half of the nineteenth century, with the appearance of the Meiningen Ensemble, led by Georg II, Duke of Saxe-Meiningen, that methods of stage production were transformed, giving 'the stage director a power and a responsibility that he had never before possessed'.[11] Hugely influential among the artists of the period, such as André Antoine, Otto Brahm, Constantin Stanislavski and Max Reinhardt, among others, the highly elaborate performances staged by the Duke of Saxony's theatre were the foundation stone for *theatre direction* being seen as a task that began to be carried out by people who separated this particular field from the creativity of the other stage professions, such as playwriting and design in particular. Directors began to have their own space, to turn their work into an art in itself.

Theatre underwent a substantial transformation from the moment when the tasks of the author (the text, the libretto) and of the director (the play as a whole, the acting, the space etc.) separated into two distinct practices and the place of the theatre director became present in all systems of theatre production. From the twentieth century onwards, the theatre director becomes an indispensable figure in the creation of the scenic act.

Today, there are many authors who direct their own plays, but this relationship is no longer the same as it was in past times. Rather, it has now been altered by the distinction that lies between the two tasks. The lack of fixed patterns in systems of production today forces us to rethink the difference between the playtext and the mise en scène. And this, of course, enriches the theatre.

---

[11]Braun, Edward, *The Director and the Stage* (London: Methuen, 1982), p.21.

Who directs?

The work of direction is rooted in deciding what orientation the various components of a mise en scène will take. This task is usually taken on by one particular person. But in reality, a show is directed by whichever person or *thing* makes most of the decisions. And these decisions are not necessarily made by people with the title of director.

When putting on a show, there are so many factors in play that it is practically impossible for just one person to decide everything. In all systems of production, from the most artistic to the most commercial, there exists a range of elements that have already been determined even before the decision has been taken to begin, and which have a remarkable effect in shaping any production. Of course, it is not impossible for one person to make all of the decisions regarding everything that makes up a production, but this does not guarantee that the result will be effective in theatrical terms.

In some state-run theatres in the Argentine provinces, where there are permanent ensembles, it is generally the actors, who have earned these public positions through an official application process and shelter within these comfort zones until the moment they retire, who make the decisions about the repertoire, choose the directors as they please and even decide how many performances there will be of each show. Shaped in this way, the *structure of the permanent ensemble*, a type of organism absolutely indispensable for a repertory theatre and for carrying out large projects, is denigrated. State bureaucracy allows for many actors to survive in these ensembles who are not in any condition to act reliably and this permanence is generally due to a misconstrued idea of job stability. When it comes to casting a particular play, it is common for there to be actors who are too old for some characters or who lack the necessary talent or skill to perform a large role. One of the most evident failings in this kind of organization is the absence of permanent directors, who are not part of the company. The directors are called once the plays have been selected or the roles have already been cast. Directing a play in the bosom of an organization of this kind means battling with many previously made decisions that are not always the best ones for putting together a show according to artistic criteria.

For many years, in the national or municipal theatres in the city of Buenos Aires, the artistic directors of these organizations functioned as the true architects of their shows. They not only selected the plays, but also chose the actors some time before hiring the person who would be responsible for directing the production. The most important decisions were left in the hands of those running the institution, leaving very little space for those responsible for shaping the performance. This process is neither good nor bad in itself. Some artistic directors of state-run theatres could be enormously creative programmers, and their decisions were very coherent when combining a text with a director and a particular cast. In other cases, decisions were taken somewhat haphazardly and this prevented the theatres from functioning properly.

In the commercial theatre, private producers tend to choose the plays, very often on the basis of shows being successful in other countries (it is very rare for plays by Argentine writers to be premiered on this circuit). In addition, given that most of these producers are generally the owners of the spaces where the plays will be performed, they decide what type of relationship the audience will have with the play, almost regardless of the kind of material chosen. And of course, they suggest and impose certain actors, especially those who will play the lead roles. Directors are generally hired after those actors whom the producer considers to be a 'draw' have been selected.

In this system of production, it is very rare for any sequence to be followed other than the one above. Directors, once on board, can choose some of the supporting actors, and sometimes their collaborators in terms of design, lighting, music and so on, but even here it is true that there are some producers who will try to impose their own people.

Although it may seem strange, even in these conditions, which hardly seem favourable for developing creative work, it is still possible to do a good job. It is a case of the director taking into account all of the variables that were decided without their choosing and making them work together to bring the show to the stage in the most effective way.

In 2006 I was asked to direct Arthur Miller's *Death of a Salesman* in the Pablo Picasso Theatre at the Teatro La Plaza, Buenos Aires, with the great Alfredo Alcón in the role of Willy Loman. This wonderful text contains a very precise indication about the design: the Loman house, with its backyard, which is, in addition, the great theme of the play. One must remember the final scene when, after Willy Loman's death, during the funeral, his wife, Linda, says:

> I made the last payment on the house today. Today, dear. And there'll be nobody home. *(A sob rises in her throat.)* We're free and clear. *(Sobbing more fully, released.)* We're free. *(Biff comes slowly toward her.)* We're free ... We're free ...[12]

According to the text, this house, with a ground floor, first floor and flat roof, is present throughout, even though there are scenes that do not take place in the house, such as those in the hotel, in Stanley's office, or in the bar in Act Two.

It is obvious that the play was written for a proscenium arch theatre with a stage that allows for the vertical construction of those two levels. One detail: above the kitchen, says the stage direction, two metres up, is the sons' bedroom. However, in this case the space chosen by the producers for the season was the Pablo Picasso Theatre, a theatre with a tendency to the semi-circular, with a low roof and raked seating, on whose stage it is practically impossible to build a second level without being squashed against the ceiling. Along with the designer Jorge Ferrari, with whom I had been working for more than fifteen years on the widest range of shows, we managed to work around this limitation and created a space in which the play could unfold narratively without losing anything of its original intention. The set was composed of a grey carpeted lawn that covered the floor of the whole stage, two grey side walls, an

---

[12]Miller, Arthur, *Death of a Salesman* (London: Penguin Classics, 2015), p. 112.

upstage wall that slid aside to reveal images of Brooklyn, buildings and offices and, in the final scene, cypress trees lost in the fog. The props were reduced to just the Lomans' bed, and four chairs. There was no need to include the kitchen or the deep-freeze, or the first floor, or the sons' beds. The space, which had been decided arbitrarily and not for artistic reasons by the producers, instead of working against the work of the direction, gave us the opportunity to propose something different to what we would have done if we had had a space with similar characteristics to those in the original stage directions.

But it is not always possible to turn the limitations that arise as a result of other people's decisions into something truly creative. This is especially the case if the organization of rehearsals does not correspond to the artistic needs of the materials but rather to 'collective working agreements' – unionized working patterns that take precedence over any other requirement that the play may have. One striking experience was the one I had while directing an opera, when I had to accept that part of the show would in effect be directed by the agreement regulating the work of the singers in the permanent chorus of the Teatro Colón in Buenos Aires.

During the 1990s, the regulation relating to the work of the chorus of this municipal theatre stated that this 'corps' [sic] could only do twelve 'services', a strange word to describe choral rehearsals. Each one of these 'services' could last no more than two hours. But not a continuous two hours, because the 'service' should include a break of about fifteen minutes for a rest. A simple calculation shows that the nominal twenty-four hours of rehearsals with the chorus are reduced to approximately twenty hours. A rehearsal time of this length could be considered fairly sufficient if the chorus's involvement in an opera is not very extensive, for example in Mozart's Così fan tutti, where the chorus is not only small, but also only makes three appearances, all of which are very short compared with the opera as a whole. Something similar occurs in Verdi's Rigoletto, where the appearances of the chorus are not extensive.

But when all the members of the chorus of an opera house, who number more than 100, have to be onstage almost throughout, such as in Sergei Prokoviev's War and Peace, this regime becomes an impediment to any kind of serious work.

The opera I had been hired to direct was Pompeyo Camps's *La oscuridad de la razón*, based on the play of the same name by the great Argentine playwright Ricardo Monti. In this opera, the chorus is onstage almost the whole time, for approximately three hours, not counting the *entr'actes*. Without paying much attention to how much time I had, I had used eighteen hours of the time allotted to the rehearsals with the chorus, which the soloists also took part in, to put together the first two acts in full. But when I came to stage the final act, which lasts one and a half hours and in which a male chorus and a female chorus intervene separately on either side, I discovered that I only had two 'services' left with which to choreograph all the movement in this final act.

I asked the theatre's rehearsal management department to give me more time to work with the chorus, something that was rejected without any consideration. They were not willing to accept my demands and I had to make do with what there was. With the stern glare of the union rep on my back, who was not going to let the members of the chorus remain for one additional minute in the rehearsal without claiming overtime, and already despairing at the impossibility of doing the work properly, I started to throw together the movement design of a one-hour act in two hours, including the demarcation of space and the scenic-performative arc of the entire act. So I jettisoned practically all of the ideas I had had for the staging of this act and had the male chorus enter from both sides of the stage and stand motionless on the terraces that formed part of the set. At a given point in the score, the chorus members had to exit the stage in the shortest time possible. I then gave the same instructions to the female chorus, who came in from behind the set and spread out over the steps of an enormous central staircase until the apotheotic finale. I gave all of the instructions at great speed, to the point that we managed to get through the whole act and there was even time left over that allowed some of the chorus members to leave earlier than planned. Satisfied, they thanked me for this gesture. They thought it was the marker of someone skilled enough to direct in that theatre: I seemed to be a *régisseur* who understood how things ought to be done: easily, quickly and with few complications. I was grateful to escape that rehearsal alive.

Once the opera had opened, a music critic from a Buenos Aires newspaper wrote that the mise en scène, in particular the movement of the chorus, was static, lacking the necessary movement and so on. The critic, who after all was only analysing what he could see, blamed me for this stasis, this lack of complexity in the construction of the piece. I could never explain to him that part of my scenic work was decided by the working agreement, which had 'directed' these parts of the opera.

The example of the opera was the one that made me think about the many elements that have to be considered when creating a mise en scène, especially in institutions where so many decisions have already been made beforehand and where it is very difficult to have full freedom. The idea of the director being free of all pressures and deciding every last detail of a show is almost a romantic illusion. Nevertheless, it seems to me that these limitations are not the real problem. All great theatre, dance and opera directors have always worked with restrictions and have still been able to make artistic decisions, taking into account both economic factors, such as space, and those imposed both by producers of commercial theatres and by the 'kings' of the state-run theatres, by the famous actors and by those who appoint permanent ensembles. Not to mention the shortages in fringe theatre such as a lack of adequate rehearsal space, limited availability of the actors for rehearsals, smaller and smaller performance spaces with practically no technology; even these do not prevent a director from being able to create. It is merely a case of understanding how these limitations work, and of working with them.

The uncapturable

1.

The performing arts are uncapturable, and this is one of the basic conditions of all the art forms that exist only in the present. As in life itself, no sooner do events occur in these art forms than they are transformed into moments of history. It does not matter whether the events are transcendent or banal. This is not important. Herein lies an enormous difference with the other art forms, whose objects remain practically identical to themselves in spite of the passing of time or their partial physical deterioration. Hans Holbein's *The Ambassadors* still has its same strange composition, and *Don Quijote* is still in print, albeit in different versions or formats: nothing changes its intrinsic shape, however much different eras may read different things into it. The performing arts, however, unfold before our eyes and ears without our being able to trap them.

It is perhaps for this reason that they may be the most difficult art forms to study, making some academics despair in their attempts to capture what happens in a show: trying to tie the elements to some system of analysis – generally far removed from any artistic thought – with the goal of giving some possible explanation that can encompass it fully.

The performing arts are like history: there can be no going back to them, but it is possible to rummage through the remains that are left over from them. Historians work with documents from the past, with texts of different formats, oral accounts or images from the period – be they drawings, paintings or photographs – in order to piece together the story of the past events referred to; theatre should be thought of in the same way.

A show can leave behind a written playtext, the scripts used by the actors for the rehearsals, programmes, photographs of the performances, sound effects or specially composed music on a CD or in sheet music, and the set models and the plans for building it, as well as the costumes hanging in a dressing room or stored carefully in boxes, files of reviews, notices in newspapers or other articles written in other circumstances, and perhaps a DVD that is not particularly well recorded but is still a record in the end and can show some of the characteristics of what took place.

Theatre critics often forget they have a weapon that gives them an advantage over all those who make theatre, with the obvious exception of the playwright. While the mise en scène itself will disappear once it ceases to be on the stage, the written words produced by critics with their often churlish judgements and recorded in the print media will be left forever as a description of what took place. This is a serious – although obviously unavoidable – structural flaw in the relationship between criticism and theatre. There will never be any way of reconstructing a show, but what is written – be it a review, an academic paper or a show report – will take the place of the event that happened. Fortunately, there exist multiple written texts about the same productions, and these divergences allow whoever did not see the show at the time to have at least some room for doubt as to what it was like. Here is one example of opposing opinions of the same show.

In 1975, along with Lorenzo Quinteros, Tina Serrano and Hernán González, I staged a production that was very different to the kind of work that was typically being made at the time. Its name was *Porca miseria* and it opened in a completely experimental venue at number 400, Calle Viamonte, Buenos Aires. The first review that came out after press night had the headline 'Absence of values at the CAYC [Centro de Arte y Comunicación, the centre for art and communications]'. Penned by the famous critic Jaime Potenze, from the newspaper *La Prensa*, often merciless with those who did not conform to his models, it fired off the following in one of the review's paragraphs: '[...] this "elite" is not select. Rather, it is simply a posthumous descendent of the Torcuato di Tella University, combining exhibitionism with confusion, at least in this work of theatre which is self-defined as humorous, but is duller than reciting the one times-table.' By contrast, Gerardo Fernández wrote in the newspaper *La Opinión*: 'However, the mixture does not result in stylistic confusion. On the contrary: *Porca miseria* displays, from beginning to end, a coherence that is ultimately its trump card, explained by the fact that the experience revolves around one binding feature that pervades it, and which many more pompous aesthetic endeavours often tend to lack: humour.'

2.

Many people say that theatre is ephemeral. This is perhaps one of the most widespread definitions in the theatrical world. But if we adhere to the dictionary definition, ephemeral comes from the Greek and means 'of only one day'. Theatre, however, is not of only one day (although there are some shows that are); rather, it is a phenomenon that appears and disappears, that is there and then is not there, night after night. And this *being there and not being there* is what defines its uncapturable essence. There is no way of tying it down.

For this reason, theatre could for many years only be thought of as dramatic literature. The texts of plays were all that remained, and these, after the invention of the printing press, became 'the theatre object' par excellence, the most stable and permanent material that anyone wanting to think about theatre could rely on.

Dramatic structures have always been shaped first and foremost by systems of production, not by playtexts. But paradoxically, it is likely that the very *uncapturability* of the performing arts may have led to the idea, which some believe, of the dramatic text being the foundation for the entire structure of theatre.

In more recent times and for their own amusement, theatre historians began to call upon other kinds of documents, as well as dramatic texts, in order to think about theatre. This led to the emerging belief that shows could be reconstructed, somehow denying this fading-away that happens whenever a performance ends.

Video, digital and other recordings help us to fool ourselves with the idea that we can see and hear a show that is already over. But this is not the case: any of these recordings are but the *remains*, only allowing us to see a few traces, and never letting us relive the experience of being in the audience at *that* moment which was once the present but has now become history, even if the show happened only a few hours ago.

We can see a reconstruction of the Battle of San Lorenzo,[13] see General San Martín being saved by Cabral, the heroic private. We can even participate ourselves in the fray, wearing national or realistic costumes. But no one will ever be able truly to relive that historic moment in all its scale. Theatre works in the same way. And this makes some people nervous.

And it is in rehearsals for a show that the *uncapturability* of the performing arts is best demonstrated. Although there is no single rehearsal method that is more effective than another, because everything depends on the material being worked with, it is true that rehearsals tend to happen almost always with a dynamic that combines the time during which the play or plays are being made with the time during which one reflects about what has been done, especially what has happened in that rehearsal and about what should happen in the show in general. This period of time spent talking is an attempt to *capture* the experience that has just happened during the running of the scenes. What directors say to actors, even to the other artists involved, is usually in order to hold onto those moments that have already happened, to maintain or modify them, and above all to try to make things work better at the next rehearsal.

And these words that are spoken, these chats that take place afterwards, are only the remains, just a memorial of what has happened, what has been felt and what is remembered, but never, ever, is the object actually there.

Incredibly, theatre, an art that is created simultaneously with the presence of the audience, cannot be *made* simultaneously. A painter can step away to look at their painting, or can talk about it, and the work in progress will be there. It is very difficult to do this with a rehearsal or in a theatre performance without changing the way it functions. We have to wait until the scenes are over before we can do anything about them.

Some directors talk to their actors literally while they are rehearsing, trying to intervene in the present moment, in an almost

---

[13]Translator's note: a key battle in the Spanish-American wars of independence, 3 February 1813.

desperate attempt to participate in the development of the scenes. This is, sometimes, a good technique, especially when things are not working well and explanations made afterwards are not understood and it is better to make them in the moment, or when trying to introduce an element of surprise into an improvisation. But these moments are not truly reflective: rather, the director also *enters* into the scene, taking on a role – albeit one external to the narration – itself intervening in the events that take place.

In the shows directed by Tadeusz Kantor, the great Polish director appeared onstage, playing himself, a director watching his own work, sometimes giving instructions. His presence gave the plays a sense of the sublime (that is the word). And yet, after having watched some of his shows many times, I realized that this role was not fulfilling the effective function of an active director in the shows, because there were no significant changes from what had been done in previous performances. Like the conductor of an orchestra, his presence could modify some aspects of rhythm, but not much else. In other words, the plays were not rethought structurally as they were happening.

One of the most difficult tasks for the director is remembering exactly what has just taken place in the rehearsal and trying to find a balance between their impressions and what has actually happened in the scene. At this point, the work of directing resembles that of an *historian* of recent events: all of the data are there: the oral accounts, the protagonists, the space, but not the event itself: it disappears the moment that the scene ends.

The director's word

We directors can do nothing for ourselves. To carry out our work we invariably depend on the other artists involved in a production. Actors can say their lines, dancers can dance, writers can write their plays and musicians can compose their pieces. Many of those who participate in a mise en scène can do their work directly, with no need for any human intermediaries.

Directors, however, do not have this option. Let us order a director, suddenly, to direct: 'You: direct, now!' The most likely thing that said person will do is lift the index finger on their best hand, with the intention of giving an order, but with the even greater intention of signalling that it is they who hold the power. They can go no further than making this gesture. Useless, of course, because, in so many words, they can do nothing for themselves, unless they also take the place of actor, writer, dancer or musician.

Directors work and develop their craft only through the other participants in the making of a mise en scène. For this reason, all the fantasies of the director's absolute power are nothing more than illusions. Whatever the relationship they have with the other participants in the work – indulgent, authoritarian, laissez-faire or bastard – it matters not; unless the other participants agree to do what the director suggests, there will not be a show with any internal coherence. Only with effective agreement from all of the people participating in a piece of group work, in which there are different roles, is it possible to bring a theatre project to fruition.

Directing involves using words (or their equivalents) to try to convince everyone else that a project is possible, and that after working on it intensely it will get somewhere. But above all, words are used to sustain with conviction ideas that we directors are not even sure of ourselves.

It is perhaps for this reason that directors try to construct these images of being all-powerful, so as to hide the congenital impossibility of their doing anything for themselves.

And since the only great tool that directors have is their words (or whatever replaces them: gestures, drawings etc., but which basically mean words), what happens in the play is the result of everything that can be articulated with language.

For this reason, a director needs to be able not only to have an idea about the material they are working on, but also to transmit this idea. There is little point in a director having wonderful thoughts about theatre if they cannot communicate them to others. I am not talking here about a supposed clarity of exposition in the merely formal sense, but rather the ability to communicate with others in an effective way. In some way, the manner in which someone 'says' during the process of creating a show is directly linked to what will be presented to the audience. Of course, these forms of communication are as many as there are directors. It is not just a question of what is said; what matters is finding the way to say it. And of course, this is not only a matter of words, or at least not the mere speaking of them.

In my experience, I have not always 'said' precise words to lighting or set designers. On a number of occasions, I have simply made a gesture with my hand and this has been enough for my colleagues to understand what I was thinking and what I meant. During preparations for Brecht's *The Life of Galileo*, which we opened in 1999 in the Teatro San Martín, Buenos Aires, I was discussing with the Argentine set and costume designer Jorge Ferrari, with whom I formed a strong professional team, about the challenge of approaching a play divided into fifteen scenes that take place in locations very different to one another. Trying to explain the structure of the play, I could not stop raising and lowering my hands alternately. My words did not refer to the space, but rather to the narrative continuity of the scenes. But this movement was picked up by Ferrari, who then encapsulated it in the final production in a set design that was formed of a variety of panels, in colours alluding to the various cities mentioned in the play: blue for Venice, green for Florence and purple for Rome, leaving yellow for the moment of the carnival, where no city in particular is indicated. The panels rose and fell, also indicating the different locations where the scenes took place: Galileo's study and the great armoury in Venice, Galileo's house in Florence, the hall of the Collegio Romano in Rome and so forth.

It is the director's words that inevitably make up the mise en scène. Whether because what needed to be said has been said, or because it has not, these words flow, in both their presence and their absence, through every sinew of the mise en scène.

In many shows one can tell that the directors have not said all of the necessary words, that many things that should have been said have not been. When this happens, the mise en scène displays blatantly a whole series of mistakes. The audience is not always able to spot these errors onstage. This tension generated between the perception of a mistake and a lack of language to describe it is enough to push audiences away from theatres. But when the audience notices the mistakes and can put them into words, something is irreparably damaged. When the audience can 'say' something about these mistakes, it is because the director never did. And I do not refer only to the words not spoken by the person who nominally occupies the role of director, but to all of the people who share in the ultimate responsibility.

A director who does not speak is one who does not succeed in spotting the failings in a play with regard to sound, visuals or writing, amongst other things. And if these errors have been allowed to go unchecked, it is because whoever is directing does not know how to solve certain problems or because, even though they are aware that the problems exist, they chose instead to keep quiet about them. In both cases there were no words to transform *the material on its way to becoming* the mise en scène. In the place of the absent word, a failing appears on the stage.

At other times, the words of the director can be seen too clearly, as if they could be 'read' in the bodies of the actors, the set design or the music. It is a case in these shows of the ideas of the direction being too obvious. The director's whims (not the arbitrary things created in order to take a production forwards – I will discuss those later) are placed before everything else, as if the words of the director had done away with the text, the actors, the space and so on, branding every fragment of the mise en scène and preventing it from being able to have a life of its own.

This way of putting on a show may calm the need of some directors to be in control, to manipulate all of the elements in such a way as to make themselves present onstage at all costs, in the moment of the performance, that very space and time when they cannot be present except through the bodies of the actors, the dancers, the musicians. This is a real tragedy for these directors, because surrendering one's body is a sometimes intolerable sensation. But deep down they have the secret awareness that directing is, among other things, accepting one's own absence onstage and letting one's own body fade into the framework of the show.

Teamwork

For a little over a decade, the word *teatrista* ('theatrist'[14]) has been circulating in Argentine performing-arts circles. It is a term that should be ejected from theatre language because of its vulgar sound, and the term 'theatre artist' should be finally restored.

But how was it that this concept, which is used indiscriminately within the theatre community, came into being? Rather than from artists, it arose from the need within the academic arena to give a name to the contemporary creatives who carry out a number of different activities within a single mise en scène. According to this term, there would no longer be *just* directors, writers, actors, designers, and so forth, but rather 'theatrists', that is to say artists who write, direct, act, build the set, design the soundtrack and so on, all in a single show.

Since the use of this term first emerged, people who do one particular job in a mise en scène – that is to say, who are only directors, actors, designers, writers etc., those who are not granted the title of 'theatrists' – have ceased to have relevance within the theatre system. These unique, specific tasks have begun not to be appreciated. Instead, only those who could combine many simultaneous tasks were valued. And in academic circles, generally distanced from effective theatrical practice, the inclusion of this new category is cheerfully celebrated and considered a virtue, while any analysis critical of this accumulation of activities into one single person is rejected.

---

[14]Translator's note: this is a similar but not necessarily identical idea to the one described by the relatively new English term *theatremaker*.

In the performing arts, whatever the genre – spoken theatre, dance, musical theatre – the number of tasks that have to be carried out to make up a show are many and varied. The volume and variety of these tasks arise from the presence of the four art forms that I am continually referring to. In literature, in visual arts, in musical composition and other artistic disciplines, the work of creation is generally taken on on an individual basis. In the theatre arts, however, it is practically impossible for a show to be made by one single person. Perhaps one artist can carry out such an endeavour (it is quite common in the arena of old-style puppet shows, perhaps because of their travelling, solitary tradition), but I believe that concentrating so many tasks into one single body contradicts the collective essence of the art of theatre.

The problem with one single person carrying so many different tasks is that the discussion of ideas between *all* of the people who make a show – artists, technicians, producers or administrative staff – is lost. However much dialogue it may be possible to have with oneself, the truth is that by concentrating together so many functions, the diversity of experiences, approaches, positions and focuses of the collective of all those involved is not unleashed. In a manner of speaking, by avoiding contact between different people, politics are eliminated. And the putting-on of any show, because it is a collective action, develops through political practice; in other words, it is an action that unfolds *between* the individuals. These words by Hannah Arendt, in *What is Politics?*, are eloquent enough about the need for dialogue and confrontation in theatre practice:

> What was more important here was the experience that no one can adequately grasp anything it its full and objective reality without his peers, because there will only ever be one perspective revealed to him: that which fits with and is inherent to his own position in the world. If he wants to see and experience the world as it 'really' is, then he can only do so by understanding it as something that is shared by many people, that lies between them, separates and connects them, that appears differently to everyone and is therefore understandable only if many people talk to each other and share their opinions and perspectives. Only when we talk freely to one another does

the world that is being talked about begin to emerge, in all its objectivity and visible from all sides.[15]

Every mise en scène, whatever its method of production or aesthetic, is built based on the negotiations that take place between different people who, from within their different roles, work together to bring it into being.

Although 'theatrists' may have the illusion that they can carry out an infinite number of tasks by themselves (something they will doubtless benefit from by being paid as an actor, writer, director, designer, musical director etc.), the fact is that despite themselves they will still have to accept having interlocutors, even though they may deny this or not be able to see it.

It is remarkable how many of these people who allow themselves to be called 'theatrists' have a 'progressive', inclusive, participative, even democratic political discourse, but in their practice do precisely the opposite, keeping all of the work to themselves.

Some people justify this accumulation of different tasks in their own person by using the examples of Shakespeare, Molière and many others, who wrote, directed and acted in their shows. What they do not say – or do not know – is that in those days the idea of directing had not yet been developed. Plays were put on according to already established staging models that allowed them, even in the premieres of new texts, to respond to the forms of production of each era and country. Molière, to give an example, wrote for his actors and for specific, pre-existing spaces. As such, the task of acting and directing was to fit the new text to the prevailing forms.

A major change occurs with the emergence, in the late nineteenth century, of directors as autonomous artists, transforming the working relationships with the other artists involved, such as set designers, costume designers, lighting designers, stage composers, choreographers and so on.

From the moment when it ceased to be believed that, like before, the most important thing was to bring the dramatic text or opera to the stage just as it had been written, and people began to think

---

[15]Arendt, Hannah, *Was ist Politik?* (Munich: R. Piper GmbH & Co KG, 1993), pp. 51–2. Translation for this volume by William Gregory.

about the variety of elements that make up a mise en scène, teams began to emerge, wherein each artist had a specific area, each with its own rules, different to those of the others. Argument, confrontation, agreement and disagreement became necessary exercises in the making of any piece of theatre. Put simply, it was accepted that every mise en scène is the result of collective thinking.

Throughout the world, the best theatre, dance or opera directors have always known that doing excellent work relies on the interaction of all of the artists who participate in putting a show together. They recognize like no one else the value of different skills in the performing arts and the time that it takes for these skills to be acquired. However much it might be the name of the director that is remembered when one thinks of a show, behind every great work there are many, many artists and creators who have discussed the ideas pervading the mise en scène.

The concentration into one single person of activities as distinct as writing, acting, set design, music and so on, is not only an act of unmeasurable narcissism; it also amounts to an impoverished understanding of the very essence of theatre. Unless a person – and there are some, just as an exception – has deeply studied and practised these various skills, it is very unlikely that they would be able to possess all of this skill at an equal level, and thus to carry out all of these tasks in a balanced way.

Many actors are extraordinary improvisers, with laudable skills of verbal inventiveness, but this does not guarantee that the words that come out of their mouths constitute a successful work of literature, or that they are automatically authors of great merit. Nor will a director who works with a cast by devising effective codes of improvisation that allow for powerful dramatic situations to unfold necessarily be able to solve specific problems with text, such as the poetic and coherent use of language.

The inventiveness that can develop in a rehearsal can be very powerful. Many directors set this in motion by setting up highly emotive or hilariously funny situations. But when they set about trying to capture this material in a play, based on these methodologies, they often fail as playwrights. The show that results from these practices often demonstrates how specifically literary practice cannot be replaced by the expressiveness of the actors.

In rehearsals, actors, with the consent of directors, start using objects, furniture or costumes that are useful to them for developing their work. But these elements do not necessarily make for an interesting visual world from the artistic point of view. It is the task of the set and costume designers to discuss what is going to be seen by the audience, because it is they who are specialized in this work. The same is true of the art of lighting, where lighting something is not the same as simply illuminating it. Many directors stand in as lighting designers when all they really do is to leave the eye of the audience wanting. For each of the theatre specialisms, a similar example could be given.

General knowledge of the skills of theatre, of any given role, does not necessarily imply specific knowledge of each and every one of the other disciplines. Sometimes, quite the contrary.

Today, many playwrights turn to directing their own texts, without having trained in this art before by, for example, assisting other directors or directing texts by other authors. Playwrights who often have a polished writing technique, refined over many years, perhaps for fear of being left out of today's system of theatre production in which one can make a great deal of money by doing more than one job, surprisingly start directing their own plays. And so excellent plays open, ruined by deficient direction. In these shows there is a tremendous imbalance in the play: on the one hand, a very well-developed, complex, brilliant text from the point of view of language, and on the other, basic direction, full of errors of space, static design and flat performances, and lacking any concept of the passing of time onstage.

Very often audiences cannot put this imbalance into words, and yet they perceive it, even if reviewers or the audience themselves 'consecrate' these shows, owing more to questions of the market or of requirements unrelated to theatre than to the artistic product itself. Very often, audiences end up criticizing the text of a play, when in reality the root of the problem lies in deficient direction.

The practice of direction becomes more disconcerting the more each person working in the process of a mise en scène brings their own skills. This combination of skills, properly interconnected, respected by the direction, translates into teams that in the majority of cases are long lasting. Because, ultimately, it is teams that carry out the work in the theatre.

Directors, playwrights, actors and all the others who think they are included in the term 'theatrists', no doubt substantially increase their self-esteem, and in some cases their assets. But ultimately they impoverish what they create, making theatre that is very uninteresting and lacking in any debate outside of itself. And this lack of confrontation kills theatre.

The director and their place as spectator

There are still some directors who tend to say things like 'I'm not interested in the audience when I'm creating', or 'I always do what I feel, I work for what I like myself, and if I do what other people like, so much the better; if not, it doesn't matter'. These types of statements are common, especially in the notices issued in advance of an opening night, but they still have a trace of outdated romanticism. Regardless of what each individual may believe, it is unlikely that those people who dedicate themselves conscientiously to the theatre (and not as a mere personal pastime, concentrating on their own pleasure with no regard to any relationship with the world around them) can say that the audience is not somehow present when thinking about, and above all rehearsing, a show.

If theatre is an art defined by a sharing between the play and the audience, then the audience should in some way be present during the whole process of developing a mise en scène.

Theatre does not work in the same way as the 'deferred' arts like literature, visual arts or cinema, whose works exist independently of being read or seen. In literature, for example, the writer is not present at the moment when the reader reads their poems or their novel in the privacy of their home. In the case of theatre, this presence is structural. For this reason, the fallacy of the argument of the independence of the theatre artist from their audience is directly linked to the idea of the unrestrained power of the director.

No matter whether they are real or imagined, a theatre director can never not think about the audience. The place of the audience should be present from the moment the material to be worked on is chosen. Because if one considers that every show that is put on is a meeting with other individuals in a public arena – and not just the manifestation of the subjectivity of the director, as if the mise en scène were a bottle thrown into the sea to be found or not by an addressee; that is to say, if one does not forget that theatre is always a political entity specifically made for this meeting – it will be obvious that the work on the material must, whether directly or indirectly, take this relationship into account.

Of course, it is not a case of 'indulging' the audience, giving them what they supposedly think they want. This is something that is widespread on commercial stages, but has recently also become common on the so-called independent or fringe stage, and above all in state-run theatres: shows are developed based on hegemonic aesthetic premises produced at international festivals, or on the parameters set in the theatre metropolises of Germany or France, because these countries tend to provide money for theatre production in Latin American countries.

It is a case of building a relationship with the audience, in all of the possible ways that connections are made between people. All kinds of interaction are available, from forging a very intense agreement all the way to the most brutal confrontation, and each director can chose how to establish them. If the director does not do this, the mise en scène as a whole will decide for itself on a relationship with the audience. It must be remembered that, in theatre, any decisions not taken will inevitably still be present, and will exist whether those who ought to have taken them realize it or not.

What should never be offered to the audience as a form of relationship is boredom, in other words anything that might make them think that going to the theatre that night was a mistake and that it would have been better and more entertaining to be somewhere else.

Thinking about the audience means being able to visualize what the ideal arrangement is for the material being worked on. And without this turning into an elitist remark, the fact is that the effectiveness of a performance is ultimately linked to its finding its audience in a clearly defined time and space. The performing arts cannot wait for their ideal audience as literature or visual arts can, where the passing of time eventually leads to a successful encounter that could not take place at the time the work of art was created.

In the theatre on offer in many countries there are infinite mises en scène that have clearly been put together with no consideration for the audience. They are often aimed at the artists themselves, and perhaps at their friends and relatives. These shows are built based on secret codes, filled with information that relates exclusively to the group they belong to, like school plays that parody the chemistry teacher, the one all the students know, and whom everyone laughs at when they see one of their own playing him onstage, but where someone outside of the group would not understand the reason for the laughter. These shows remain closed in on their own musings, without any attempt to make them relevant beyond themselves. There is not even an approach to entertainment that allows someone who is not one of the 'congregation' to participate in anything going on in the play. Even shows considered cryptic in relation to theme and form contain some kind of reflection about art or society, or about the act of perception itself, that might be shared. This does not happen in shows where the audience has been forgotten.

In the daily practice of direction, the audience should be present at each and every rehearsal. And this happens when the director is aware that the place from which they are directing is the same place as that occupied by the audience. And I do not say this in the merely rhetorical sense; rather, in that it is physically the same place. The difference is that it is the director who is the most qualified audience, the one with the most technical tools and who, through words, has the ability to shape the various elements until they are transformed into a piece of theatre.

In many shows one can work out which spot in the auditorium the director did their work from. There are theatre venues which, because of their size, make it obvious whether or not the director remained seated all the time in one single spot, composing all of the scenes from that one seat, or if instead they moved around all of the possible positions in the auditorium so that they could have a relatively 'democratic' view.

A 'tragic' aspect of theatre is that it reflects eloquently the relationship each director forms with a show's possible audience. There are those who underestimate people, producing theatre that undervalues the audience's mental strength and sensitivity. Others attack the wrong audience, shouting from the stage about social and political responsibilities to people who patiently have taken the trouble of coming tonight to the theatre and who really are not the intended target of this diatribe. Others seem to turn their backs on the audience, making everything excessively incomprehensible. And there are those who are obviously exhausted and no longer have any contact with anyone. Fortunately, there are still more directors who want to establish an intense relationship with the audience, making an unforgettable night for everybody.

Danger in the performing arts

Theatre has become a *dangerous* art for the audience. And not only the theatre, but rather all of the performing arts: dance, opera, pop concerts, classical music recitals and so on.

All of those art forms that take place in the same time and space as the audience are no longer perceived in the way they were years ago. In past times, approximately until the beginning of the twentieth century, most entertainment could only be enjoyed by leaving the domestic environment. With the exception of chamber music, generally performed by family members or friends, or some theatre performances staged in theatre spaces within bourgeois mansions, other activities, such as theatre, circus and large-scale instrumental music, like symphonies, oratorios and so on, had to take place in public places to which people had no choice but *to go*.

With the advance of the twentieth century, technological developments led to industrial products that allowed access to entertainment that permitted people to stay in their homes. It was then that perceptions of the performing arts began to change.

And it is particularly in recent years, with home cinemas, video recorders, DVD players, the internet, cable television, computer games and all of the devices constantly appearing on the market from the entertainment industry, that activities that take place outside of the home have begun to be thought of as unsafe, dangerous experiences.

But what do I mean by unsafe and dangerous? Specifically, the fact that art forms that take place in the present and in the same space as the audience can be halted at any moment by external factors. The very idea that the continuity of a play might be interrupted becomes something unbearable for those present.

Audiences have enormous stamina for accepting any interruption that might occur during a performance. In many theatres, there have often been cuts in the electrical supply and as a result the stage has fallen into darkness. Clearly, this is an accident that interrupts the normal progression of the play. And yet, the audience's first reaction is to believe that this sudden blackout is part of the show. Only when someone from the theatre staff finally appears and announces that the show cannot continue owing to a lack of electricity, will the audience start to believe, albeit reluctantly, in the possibility that the performance might not go on. But a voice will always appear from among the audience suggesting that it carry on regardless: with candles, torches or with mobile-phone screens. No matter that the show has been designed almost wholly with the use of technology that depends on electricity, this fear that the stoppage has caused in the audience will only be assuaged by the idea that the show can go on by any means whatsoever. Interruption in the performing arts means the *invasion of day-to-day reality* into the fictional space. And this is intolerable for the audience. This is what is unsafe; this is the danger.

A few years ago, at the National Theatre of Spain's Teatro María Guerrero in Madrid, I saw a show produced by the Catalan company La Fura dels Baus, entitled *Boris Godunov*. The performance began a little vaguely, with scenes based on the work of the same name by Alexander Pushkin, framed by extremely high screens onto which images of Russian palaces were projected. But shortly after the show began, both on the stage and in the auditorium, an 'invasion' took place, with actors playing the roles of terrorists who 'occupied' the space by force, interrupting the supposed performance of *Boris Godunov*, in a clear allusion to the attack on the Dubrovka Theatre in 2002 in Moscow by a group of Chechen attackers and which, after the intervention of the Russian army, left more than 170 people dead, included the Chechen terrorists and members of the audience.

By this point, all of the audience had forgotten Tsar Boris and his trouble with the boyars, to concentrate on the unexpected behaviour of the actors shouting all over the Madrid theatre. From all sides, 'terrorists' appeared wielding weapons whose purpose was

obvious: machine guns, revolvers, digital timebombs and charges
of dynamite. They continually threatened the audience, shouted at
them not to move from their seats and said that anyone who dared
stand up would be executed on the spot. To demonstrate that this
threat was very serious, they suddenly grabbed an actor who was in
the auditorium playing an 'audience member', shouted a few things
at him that could not quite be understood and dragged him out of
the hall. A few seconds later, we heard a gunshot, as if he had been
shot for not respecting the orders of the terrorist bosses.

In the row behind the one I was sitting in, there was an actor
playing a 'terrorist' handling 'bombs', those ones with little blinking
lights that reminded me of children's shows from my childhood
when they were trying to show something from the future. She
was making so much noise with her actions that it was sometimes
impossible to hear parts of the show where we were supposed to be
able to hear what was being said.

I had never seen so many audience members in a theatre making
such an enormous effort to sustain a fiction that had been so badly
put together. Any audience member taking the huge decision to get
up and go to the *toilette* in the middle of the performance would
have put the entire show at risk. Obviously, no one did, because
the fear of interrupting this over-simplistic and unrealistic offering
was so great that the audience put up with anything. Unfortunately,
there was no one who grew sick enough of it to shout out, like the
child in the story, 'The Emperor's got no clothes!' Not even I dared
to, I must confess, because I was fascinated, trying to see how far
one could go with this display of artistic political opportunism.

Just as the risk of interruption in the performing arts has become
an increasingly unbearable feeling of danger, the contemporary
audience has at the same time furnished itself with the greatest
amount of apparatus around them to allow themselves the illusion
of absolute control with regard to entertainment. Thanks to
recordings, they can see their favourite programmes on a cable
channel at a time of their choosing. They handle their remote
control with dexterity, fast-forwarding or rewinding their DVDs or
pre-recorded programmes as they please. They press pause at the
least appropriate moments to go fetch a drink or leave watching
the rest of a given film until the following day. The contemporary
audience lives in the fantasy of a world they can manipulate as they
please.

Meanwhile, in the theatre (and also in the cinema) this is impossible. Chronological time moves inexorably forwards without the audience having the ability to control it. The show cannot be fast-forwarded or rewound, it cannot be stopped for a bathroom break or a phone conversation.

Theatre is an art of time which today, unlike in other times, requires an audience to put up with this lack of control. A control they enjoy daily in their homes, with domestic technology that makes them believe they can do anything with the films or the series that play on their televisions or their computers.

Today's audience is not willing to hand over its body just like that when it has the option to entertain itself in a controlled way and without fear. For this surrender to take place, for them to want to come back to the theatre, the audience needs not only to feel the pleasure of not being in its own habitat for a while, but also not to feel afraid of the invasion of the *real* during the performance.

Theatre is not like circus, where we hope to be the lucky audience that is there on the day when the trapeze artist falls to the floor with a splat. The safety net disappoints us and limits our desire to be witnesses to that extraordinary day. Theatre does not work in the same way. In fact, it is completely the opposite: the audience needs to be certain that things will be more or less the same (although not identical) to the days before. This generates a certain sense of calm (which is not the same as comfort) and trust when going to a show. So the audience allows itself to yield to the pleasure of experiencing everything that happens in the play but without losing its critical faculties, something that Brecht called for with his idea of a cigarette-smoking audience who can see everything with a certain distance.

There are many things that can stop the progress of a show and these must be worked on by the director. The director must always be aware of anything that could cause the interrupting effect of reality invading the performance, in other words all of those mistakes in approach and execution that can disrupt the play and make it lose coherence. A verbal tic of an actor that cannot be hidden, a prop or piece of scenery that does not enter or exit the stage properly, an actor who is obviously not in their light, holes in the blacks that should not be visible but are; all of these generate the effect of interrupting the flow of the show. These disruptions and all of the ones that one could add attack the attention of the audience.

Whenever they sense these malfunctions (and can recognize them), the effect of interruption is produced.

Understanding this state of 'danger' that is generated by the presence of the interrupting effect of even the smallest detail may make it easier to understand why audiences are coming less and less to any of the performing arts. Genuine audiences – in other words those who do not belong to the closest circle of those who make and produce theatre, dance or musicals, who go to see their acquaintances' or relatives' shows without too much reflection – are enormously brave, having to withstand the fear that everything could be destroyed in an instant without their being able to run away.

Speaking as audience members, is there anything as horrible as that moment when we are totally engrossed in what is happening in the play and suddenly, because of some event that cannot be hidden, the flow of the play is cut off? The fiction suddenly dies, plunging the audience into the profoundest of disappointments. It is something we often think of as irreparable. For this reason, the audience is always generous; often too much so. They notice the mistake onstage, but having left their house, bought a ticket and sat down in their seat to see a show, they will take a long time to acknowledge these interruptions: the only thing this would achieve would be to ruin an evening that was supposed to guarantee some theatrical pleasure.

During a performance of *King Lear* that I directed in the Teatro Apolo in 2009, almost at the end of Act Four, an audience member collapsed in the auditorium. It seemed he was not at all well and the people with him began to call, first quietly and then loudly, for help for the sick man. This situation inevitably caused the show to be halted. The actors who were onstage at that time stopped in surprise and watched as the house lights came on in the hall. Members of theatre staff quickly came into the auditorium and took charge of the anxious situation that was unfolding, attending to the sick man and his companions. Closely behind them, paramedics arrived to check over the audience member who was having difficulties. As they were doing so, they realized that he was in a serious condition and needed to be transferred to the ambulance they had arrived in. Having rushed into the auditorium with such urgency, they had not brought a stretcher with them for the transfer. One of them could think of nothing better than to borrow from the stage one of the five long aluminium benches that were being used as the only props in the mise en scène. They used this to carry the audience member who had been taken ill quickly from the theatre.

In the auditorium there was an enormous sense of relief that the situation had finally resolved itself, but one could also sense a huge discomfort that the performance had been interrupted. Proof of this was that no one, none of those present, showed even the slightest sign of getting up from their seat. A few minutes after the paramedics had left with the patient, the assistant director came out and said that the performance was going to start again from the beginning of the interrupted scene. Before leaving the stage, which now had one less bench than required, he remarked to the audience that he had just learned that the audience member who had been taken ill had recovered from his difficulties and was now in perfect health. The auditorium sighed, relieved, applauded the news and settled down to watch and hear how the story of this king gone mad continued.

At the end of the performance, I asked the assistant director how he had found out about the patient's state of health. As if it were perfectly natural, he told me that in actual fact he had never heard anything, that the patient might have recovered or might have died. It had occurred to him to say it at the time, because it seemed to him he needed to calm the audience down somehow, even though it was a lie, so that the show could go on.

Asking questions

Whenever the goal is to stage a show with any artistic intent, the work of the director should contain a question to be answered during the rehearsal process. It does not matter what the question is, because when it comes to directing there are many.

Heiner Müller says it clearly: 'Theatre is only interesting when you don't know what you're doing'.[16]

This not knowing of Müller's does not refer, of course, to not possessing basic theatrical tools. Although it is true that directing is generally learned by doing, it is also true that when approaching a task with any sense of artistic responsibility, rather than with a fly-by-night attitude, a director must first have developed a number of skills. This allows the director to detect the questions that will make for a mise en scène that other people will find very interesting.

At the beginning of a project, little is known about which direction a particular piece of work will take. And this position of not knowing is what truly drives the work of putting this new show together.

These questions may refer to the aesthetic, the social, the philosophical or the theatrical in its stricter sense, and should allow for a new perspective to be opened up in the audience's horizons.

Clearly, when I talk of questions holding a piece of work together I do not mean a lack of understanding of technical matters that should be basic knowledge.

---

[16]Quoted in Hornigk, Frank; Linzer, Martin; Raddatz, Frank; Storch, Wolfgang; and Teschke, Holger (eds), *Kalkfell Für Heiner Müller – Arbeitsbuch* (Berlin: Theater der Zeit, 1996), p. 141. Translation for this volume by William Gregory.

It is sometimes striking that some directors, young or old, say they are researching such-and-such an aspect of theatre when in truth they are trying to learn how to do something that theatre and its techniques have known about for quite some time. If the theatre is to develop as an art form, directors would do well not to start their work by walking along already well-trodden paths. Instead, they should start from the point of inflection between what already exists and the void awaiting the emergence of something different.

Walking along well-known paths is a very good exercise in the training of directors but not the best for putting work in front of an unprotected audience who will not necessarily understand that what is happening onstage is part of a director's apprenticeship. One thing that stops many people from going to the theatre is the fact that what is being offered to them has already been offered to them an infinite number of times before. Although there are many audiences who prefer not to stray from what they already know, there are, fortunately, many others who do want to go to a show that moves them in many senses, and this being moved that they hope for is directly connected to the questions contained in the mise en scène.

The quote from Müller refers, at least as far as I understand it, to everything that is not immediately obvious in the material being worked on and to how, by generating questions in the preparatory work, in the rehearsals and even during the performances, something will be allowed to emerge that is different from what has been done before.

Whatever the questions that may arise during the process of the building of the mise en scène, it is good to make them clear, to share them with the whole team in order to make them aware of these questions in every moment of the process, because these questions are in some way what shapes the whole work of direction.

These questions, which will flow through the entire work, are in every sinew of the mise en scène. It is thanks to them that a meaningful connection is formed with the audience, involving them and prompting them to have questions of their own. This, in turn, will lead to their committing to the play as a whole.

Unfortunately there are more and more shows that ask no new questions of their material, or that ask themselves nothing about theatre, about the audience or about human behaviour. Many of these shows – especially in the sector that has a social duty to ask as many questions as possible about art – tirelessly repeat formulas of work, producing shows with no questions at all.

In the aforementioned version of *King Lear*, one of my questions (although not the only one) was to try to understand how I should work on such a complex play, one which demands an enormous effort of concentration from the audience, with a terribly confusing plot – perhaps one of the most famous of Shakespeare's works that is least easily understood on a first reading – and succeed in the audience being able to grasp in a very simple way, during the performance, not only the plot but also the poetic level of the play.

On one hand the audience might come to the theatre attracted by a powerful publicity campaign in various media, but mainly because of the attraction that the profile of as beloved an actor as Alfredo Alcón has always had for the Argentine public. On the other they may not be sure of what was being offered to them, given that these kinds of plays, Shakespearean tragedies, are not normally staged on the commercial circuit (where it is more usual to stage light comedies or contemporary titles in the style of Broadway or the West End), but more usually in a state-run venue.

The show, in this commercial theatre space, had already caused some friction by challenging certain venues considered previously as having 'cultural' repertoires. So-called 'cultured' theatre, thought of as boring or didactic in the worst sense of the word, tends to be the territory of state-run venues, whereas theatre for entertainment is thought of predominantly as the realm of the commercial circuit. Based on this tension, between what happens in the play (which did not yield to any pressure to make the material less heavy, something impossible with *King Lear* because death and horror are present from the beginning) and this space not originally intended for these shows, the question of how people would understand such a play had pervaded all of the work in the rehearsals and was in the bodies of the actors. By posing this question, a mechanism was activated, making the audience much more active in its participation and allowing it to follow the story with ease. The emotion that ran through the auditorium at the end of the show, at the sight of Lear's pain at the death of Cordelia, showed that the audience had understood the show perfectly, and had not witnessed a mere *cultural event* – that phenomenon where the public consumes culture without it leaving the slightest mark on them – but rather a unique aesthetic experience.

Simultaneity

Theatre directors must develop a very complex skill: the simultaneous handling of all of the elements set into motion during the process of staging a show.

Unlike the other art forms, in which works can be made in a non-progressive way, and where the artist works on one concrete material – writers with language, visual artists with images etc. – in the performing arts the materials handled by the director become geometrically more complex and more numerous as the work progresses.

Although there are no fixed rules for establishing what these processes of work should be like, it is fairly likely that at the beginning of a production one can go step by step, from the simplest thing to the most complex, from the small to the large, from the dispersed to the concentrated, incorporating these difficulties one by one. If they were all considered at the very beginning, they would prove impossible to handle. But inevitably in rehearsals there comes a moment where one needs an idea of the whole in order to be able to consider the totality of the object that is being created. An overall idea that allows the process to continue advancing and incorporating all its elements.

It is practically impossible to detect the problems in the construction of a play, and from there to apply the necessary solutions, if there is not minute and above all simultaneous attention paid to the details of each element and their relationship to the whole.

Over the years, almost without realizing, I began to develop a sort of 'suspended attention' that allows for my attention to 'walk across' not only the detail but also the entirety of what is happening in a play.

This mechanism is somewhat similar to the technique used by psychoanalysts to listen to what they are analysing. In one of his works of psychoanalytic technique, Sigmund Freud writes:

> The technique, however, is a very simple one. As we shall see, it rejects the use of any special expedient (even that of taking notes). It consists simply in not directing one's notice to anything in particular and in maintaining the same 'evenly suspended attention' (as I have called it) in the face of all that one hears. In this way we spare ourselves a strain on our attention which could not in any case be kept up for several hours daily, and we avoid a danger which is inseparable from the exercise of deliberate attention. For as soon as anyone deliberately concentrates his attention to a certain degree, he begins to select from the material before him; one point will be fixed in his mind with particular clearness and some other will be correspondingly disregarded, and in making this selection he will be following his expectations or inclinations. This, however, is precisely what must not be done. In making the selection, if he follows his expectations he is in danger of never finding anything but what he already knows; and if he follows his inclinations he will certainly falsify what he may perceive. It must not be forgotten that the things one hears are for the most part things whose meaning is only recognized later on.[17]

In clinical psychoanalysis the use of this technique is suggested as a way of approaching listening; in the theatre the director should, then, have an equivalent attitude, but in relation to all the elements of the play. This involves much more than listening alone: the bodies of the actors and their relationship to the overall space, the dramatic situation in the present of the play, the speaking of the words in every rehearsal, the aspects of design and their relationship to the lighting and so forth. From within this tangle of such different

---

[17]Freud, Sigmund, 'Recommendations for Physicians on the Psycho-Analytic Method of Treatment', trans. Joan Riviere and James Strachey, in Strachey, James; Freud, Anna; Strachey, Alix; and Tyson, Alan (eds and trans), *The Standard Edition of the Complete Psychological Works of Sigmund Freud: Volume XII (1911–13) The Case of Schreber, Papers on Technique and Other Works* (London: Hogarth Press and the Institute of Psychoanalysis, 1958), pp. 111–12.

components, the director must be able to choose, each time, at each rehearsal, which of them present the most important problems, in order to work on them, specify them and isolate them for a few moments in order to be able to change them. The director also needs to be able to detect when there are elements missing that for some reason were not thought of before and are not present in the play. Thanks to this suspended attention it is possible for these gaps to become obvious.

If the material being worked on has some problem that has been identified as the most complicated one to resolve – an actor who does not understand the situation, the difficulty of this story 'fitting into' this particular space etc. – the 'suspended attention' suggests not concentrating one's attention on this problem in particular, but rather letting the object itself, this *something* that is being made, reveal all of it shortcomings as the rehearsals go on. The solution will eventually make itself clear, to the director and to the team: the actor will finally understand the situation or will leave the cast, and the story will fit into the space or it will move to another theatre.

Just as marble guides its sculptor to find the right shape, in the same way a show, once its working methods and internal laws have been established, will show where it works and where it does not, where there is a need to add something or where something is surplus to requirements.

Noticing these different events that take place simultaneously in rehearsals and then trying to remember them is a way of training suspended attention. For this, one needs to leave aside the idea of concentration in the traditional sense, the one that says that one needs to focus all one's attention onto one single thing. Suspended attention – which we could also call 'divergent' attention – works in the opposite way. It allows us to be aware simultaneously of the large amount of information of different kinds that is produced in a rehearsal, in order to be able to solve the problems of the mise en scène.

Art or entertainment

The performing arts have grown more complex ever since the field of theatre production was sharply divided into two territories: on the one hand, the commercial system, which sought an immediate economic return, and on the other, the system that aimed to be artistic, with purely cultural, non-commercial aims. As a result of this division, the concepts of art on one hand and fun or entertainment on the other have often been left on opposite sides of the road.

Perhaps because of this it is no bad thing to recall again the texts of Brecht's *Short Organum for the Theatre* (1948) in which he expresses his ideas about theatre and entertainment. Here are a few fragments:

1

Theatre consists in this: making live representations of reported or invented happenings between human beings and doing so with a view to entertainment. At any rate that is what we shall mean when we speak of theatre, whether old or new.

2

To extend the definition we might add happenings between humans and gods, but as we are only seeking to establish the minimum we can leave such matters aside. Even if we did accept such an extension we should still have to say that the 'theatre' set-up's broadest function was to give pleasure. It is the noblest function that we have found for 'theatre'.

[...]

5

Even when people speak of higher and lower degrees of pleasure, art stares impassively back at them; for it wishes to fly high and low and to be left in peace, so long as it can give pleasure to people.

6

Yet there are weaker (simple) and stronger (complex) pleasures which the theatre can create. The last-named, which are what we are dealing with in great drama, attain their climaxes rather as cohabitation does through love: they are more intricate, richer in communication, more contradictory and more productive of results.

7

Different periods' pleasures varied naturally according to the system under which people lived in society at the time. The Greek *demos* [literally: the demos of the Greek circus] ruled by tyrants had to be entertained differently from the feudal court of Louis XIV. The theatre was required to deliver different representations of men's life together: not just representations of a different life, but also representations of a different sort.

[...]

10

For all of the many sorts of representation of happenings between humans which the theatre has made since ancient times, and which have given entertainment despite their incorrectness and improbability, there are even today an astonishing number that give entertainment to us.[18]

---

[18]Brecht, Bertolt, *A Short Organum for the Theatre*, trans. John Willet, in *Brecht on Theatre* (London: Methuen, 1974), pp. 180–2 (2nd ed.).

For Brecht and his era, entertainment may be defined variously as 'weak' or 'strong', but art never falls outside of these categories. Today, on the other hand, across all social groups, regardless of their level or type of capitalist development, and in the various contexts of theatre and cultural production, it has come to be accepted as the *dominant common-sense view* that artistic work is only present in state-run, independent or fringe theatres, while entertainment is produced exclusively on the commercial circuit.

I think that it is a mistake to continue thinking this way. Not only is the idea highly prejudiced, it also does not correspond to what is really happening in theatres. Productions staged in commercial theatres sometimes contain moments that, albeit fleeting, are profoundly artistic and of course entertaining, while at some shows in state-run or fringe venues one can sometimes glimpse not one single minute of art. In other words, shows with no artistic pretensions whatsoever can sometimes be more aesthetically sophisticated than productions that call themselves artistic.

Barely a month before the coup d'état that imposed the worst dictatorship of Argentine history, in the year 1976, I was with some colleagues at a show staged in a circus tent on the outskirts of the city of Chivilcoy, in Buenos Aires province.

The company staging the show was one of the latest exponents of what was known as 'circus with a second half', but unlike the large circuses that had toured the country combining circus acts with plays, this troupe performed circus acts that were rather poor, owing to a general decline back then in circus as a genre. The theatre performance that was presented in the second half, however, caused the way in which the entire phenomenon was thought about to shift its perspective.

The company had a repertoire of different titles, which they alternated in the different places where they toured, so they might perform *Juan Moreira*, their little gaucho warhorse, or *The Kiss of Death*, a moral drama about the ravages of syphilis on young people.

The play that was performed on the day we went was a classic from Argentina's most populist theatre, *How Nice it is to be Married and Have Your Mother-in-Law Next-Door*, a farcical comedy by a fairly prolific author named Juan Carlos Muello, which had originally been premiered in the late 1950s, doubtless by a company with a leading lady much beloved by the audiences of that kind of theatre. In the 1970s, this play was no longer part of any repertoire, not even in theatres in the commercial system; it had become an exponent of a playwriting style which, at that time, was by then being used in 'theatre' programmes on television, like *Teatro como en el teatro* ('Theatre like in the Theatre') or *El teatro de Dario Vittori* ('The Theatre of Dario Vittori').

In a rather threadbare tent, opposite the entrance to the oval circus tent, was a stage that was used for the play. It was rectangular, with a small, very makeshift curtain covering the stage. After the inevitable interval following the circus first-half, we settled down to watch the promised play. The first thing of note was that the cast had been reduced to the most important characters from the original work, because it had been adapted to the capacity of this circus troupe. The version retained only the essential characters from Muello's play: the father, the mother, the daughter, the son and the bridegroom.

With scant resources, the play told the timeless story of the theatre popular in the nineteenth and early twentieth century: a mother-in-law, generally a woman of very bad character simply by virtue of being the mother of the bride, makes life impossible for her son-in-law. This circus's version had not only reduced the number of characters, but had also changed some of their characteristics: while in the original play the protagonist, the father in question and husband to the mother-in-law of the title, is the son of Italians who speaks 'cocoliche', a slang typical of the Argentine theatre that imitates Italians resident in the country, in this mise en scène the character had lost his condition of being descended from immigrants.

With practically no design elements, what was striking from the beginning of the show was the level of violence unfolding onstage and how directly and brutally it was expressed. It was as if the circus arena gave them permission for the bestial, for a complete break from any form of bourgeois theatre.

In those days, there was no cult of circus in our country, not even of clowning. (This happened from the start of the 1980s, when clowning, buffoonery and circus skills courses started to be taught in specifically theatre arenas.) For this reason, what was happening onstage was profoundly original, coming from the theatre and circus traditions of the nineteenth century and in no way reflecting the new artistic theatre tendency. Clowning took its place comprehensively in its place of origin: the circus.

The pure intuition of the artists, but also the accumulation of acting experiences developed through constant contact with the audiences of the different venues that they tended to tour, had led them to develop ways of acting that were filled with meaning: during one scene in which the entire family gathered to eat, the mother, by now fighting with her entire family, before serving the meal, showed clearly to the audience how she wiped the plates on her backside without the other characters seeing. This done, she placed a slice of ham on the plate and offered it to each of the diners, who gobbled down the ham voraciously.

Such a level of synthesis in the representation of a society, which was becoming more and more violent, was not easy to find in the theatre of the period and nor, above all, was the obvious freedom with which these situations were created onstage. The comic effect was immense, the tent shook with laughter, and I remember that moment as one of the most enjoyable I have experienced in my whole life as an audience member.

It is likely, if not certain, that the makers of that show, noble travelling artists, had little idea of the tensions and artistic polemics circulating around the territories of theatre in the cities. Nevertheless, the work of this circus troupe, possessors of the expressive power of some popular artforms – many of them poorly appropriated and tamed nowadays by television – contained more artistic consideration of the relationship between play and audience than many of the shows that were being put on in the major theatres of the country's large cities. Those who attended that night laughed a great deal and also became serious, alternately, always attentive to a play that never stopped provoking them – and without art and entertainment separating for a single moment.

Tours and transfers

Tours are the expression of one of the most perverse things that exist in theatre. (Obviously not in the sexual sense; in this case, perversion would mean trying to insert an object into a place where it should not or cannot fit.)

Every mise en scène is created for a specific space, with particular dimensions that determine from the outset how practically all of the systems of expression involved – i.e the art forms in question – will work. But it is not only the purely physical spatial elements that shape the making of a show; it is also matters of an ideological nature contained in the spaces where mises en scène are created.

When a show tours, it becomes disconnected from its specific, unique place of origin, the place that was one of the main factors in shaping the whole mise en scène. This dislocation affects almost every aspect of the show even before any kind of transfer takes place, whether it be for a fresh run in a new venue or for a tour to other cities. Since it is practically impossible to find two identical spaces, when the spatial proportions change the original show is transformed into something else, often tantamount to a deformity.

It is common to see this problem at performing arts festivals. Because of an attempt to let more audiences see shows, one often sees productions that were created for small spaces, with a level of detail that requires great intimacy, transferred to enormous venues. At the other extreme, mises en scène that require an open space, with lots of 'air' around them, find themselves cooped up in theatres that do not allow them to spread out as they did in their original spaces.

During the 1999 Buenos Aires International Festival, Romeo Castelluci's *Oresteia* was staged. The play had premiered at the

Teatro Fabbricone in Prato, Italy – a repurposed former factory, hence its name – four years before this run at the Martín Coronado Theatre at the Buenos Aires Complejo Teatral, a space designed by Mario Roberto Álvarez in the 1950s using all of the basic parameters of theatre architecture for a space for 1,200 people: end-on stage, soft seating, wooden décor, a nice, bourgeois space. Although I had not seen the original production, one could sense a certain contradiction between the show and the space it was now housed in. This venue imposed a level of stiffness and solemnity which, clearly from what was happening in the play, was not part of what the show intended. The ideas presented by Castellucci could still be seen, but many of them were diminished thanks to the seats in this Buenos Aires theatre allowing the audience to sink into them, generating a level of comfort that allowed them to resist the violence of the show.

Shortly after leaving the show I began to ask why the organizers of the festival had not sought out a huge shed to present this tremendously disquieting show in, not only because of its images, but also because of its relationship to space. In Buenos Aires it would not have been very difficult to reproduce some features, perhaps the essential ones, of the original space: the effects of neoliberalism had already left their ravages on the economy and the city was full of empty factories, and with careful reconditioning a venue that was close to the original proposition could have been created. It was clear that the show needed, from its deep structure, a space not originally built as a theatre, to transmit all of the aesthetic and ideological power of the mise en scène like the one that had been premiered in that Italian theatre.

It goes without saying that I am not suggesting that mises en scène should remain immobile in their original venues without going out to new spaces. Despite all of the alterations that are produced by tours and festivals, one can still see wonderful shows outside of their original spaces and in some cases the new spaces can even illuminate aspects of the show that the original version had not taken into account. It is just a case of being very aware of the way in which new venues can alter, deform and even betray the original make-up of a mise en scène and of how, based on this awareness, one can make the necessary modifications so that the show can closely resemble its original form.

The example of *Oresteia* is still noteworthy, because artists of great prestige and power in the international theatre world tend to demand for their productions at festivals spaces similar to those of their original performances. I remember *Ubu*, directed by Peter Brook, in its run at the Caracas International Theatre Festival, in 1978. The shows took place in an old cinema in the city, which was being used as a garage. Although the building was different in many ways, after a few alterations were carried out, such as the blocking-up of some vehicle access doors that had been put in when the building had ceased to be used as a cinema, the space bore a remarkable resemblance to Les Bouffes du Nord, the company's home in Paris, especially in the way that the audience related to the play and in the roughness of the space, something indispensable for that production.

There are some directors who take their pretensions too far and even demand that spaces be built for them that are practically the same as the ones where their shows premiered.

But not all creators are in a position to demand spaces adequate for their transfers. Often, the assigned venues are practically the opposite of what is needed. A few years ago, I toured to Madrid and Berlin with Ingrid Pelicori, Horacio Peña and Pablo Caramelo with a production of *The Library of Babel*, a show based on the text by Jorge Luis Borges, which I co-directed with Edgardo Rudnitzky and which had premiered in the Biblioteca Miguel Cané, in the Buenos Aires neighbourhood of Boedo. Borges had worked in this old library as a book cataloguer in the early 1940s. The setting of the library, slightly decaying, with its smell of old wood and peeling walls, was the ideal space for staging the show. Although the building was not set up for housing the performing arts, still the actors and the audiences clung to this 'theoretical fiction', which had nothing theatrical about it. The same tables used by the library's usual readers for their reading were used now by the actors. A few seats placed at these tables in front of the shelves filled with the library's own books were the place assigned to the audience.

Our dramatized version staged the entirety of Borges' text, with its story, epigraph and footnotes told by the librarians, a man and a woman, old bureaucrats, dressed in the same overalls that the venue's employees used. Meanwhile, an actor-reader, who earlier had read some fragments referring to the narrative that could now be heard (extracts from the *Autobiography*, written in English with the collaboration of Norman Thomas di Giovanni) reads the book in silence. The librarians, almost nonchalantly, perhaps mimicking Borges' workmates at the library, who were sometimes surprised to find the author's namesake in an encyclopaedia, explained to some unlikely visitors (the audience) how it was that 'The universe (which others call the Library) is composed of an indefinite, and perhaps infinite, number of hexagonal galleries.'[19]

Whether one has read him or not, Borges is an author who is very well known and well respected by the general public in Argentina and it was quite likely that the audience who came to see our show felt attracted as much by the text as by the opportunity to spend a little under an hour in the same place where Borges had worked. The show was made powerful not only by the shape of the space but also because of that place's symbolic power.

It proved practically impossible to find any of these characteristics in the spaces where we performed during the tour of Spain and Germany, despite the efforts and goodwill of those who organized the trip. In Madrid, the chosen building was the legendary and historic Biblioteca Nacional de España, seemingly an ideal place for the performance of Borges' story. Unfortunately we were not allowed to perform in any of the reading rooms. Instead, we had to perform in a kind of lecture theatre, a very modern space within an old building, with a projection screen at the back wall. In this space, it was impossible for the ideas of the mise en scène to circulate and as the show progressed the meanings of the text that had been obvious in the library back in Boedo began to disappear. Despite the enormous efforts of the talented actors to try to restore them, to unleash them, their bodies and voices faded in an environment that was ultimately hostile.

In Germany, in both Cologne and Berlin, the show could take place amongst shelves and books, but both libraries were relatively modern; there was nothing in them of the deterioration of the public building so typical of our country and so necessary for the

[19]Borges, Jorge Luis, 'La biblioteca de Babel', in *El jardín de senderos que se bifurcan* (Buenos Aires: Ediciones Sur, 1942), p. 93. Translation for this volume by William Gregory.

mise en scène to be understood without having to give too many explanations. Although it was a little closer to the original idea, it was still not possible to achieve the same spirit intended in the original show. I always thought the ideal thing would have been to build a reconstruction of the Biblioteca Miguel Cané on a slightly smaller scale, within another space. But the budgets for our company could not run to such an investment.

In an attempt to mitigate this distance between the new space and the original, we hired Magdalena Viggiani, an excellent photographer, to prepare a series of photographs of the library in Boedo. Placed in the entranceways to the performance spaces, these images allowed the audience to have some remote idea of the space before the show started. A by now desperate attempt to recover something that had inevitably been lost already.

The experience was very different with a production of *The Love of Don Perlimpín and Belisa in his Garden* by Federico García Lorca, which we staged a couple of years after the Borges project. From the beginning of the project we already knew that the show would tour many of the public libraries of the city of Buenos Aires, spaces in no way fitted out as theatre venues and which varied enormously in shape. We would open in one of them, but the following weekend we would have to begin touring almost every neighbourhood in the city. Practically none of these libraries had been purpose-built, generally they were refurbished old houses, and one of them had even been a commercial unit in the lower floors of an apartment block. The variety of spaces that lay before us meant that we would have to contend with very different rooms, and at best some form of platform would be erected to raise the performance area so that the audience, generally seated in rows all on one level, would be able to see a little better.

The main challenge was to design a mise en scène that could be adaptable to any space and that would not be excessively distorted during its tour through the various libraries.

From the outset, as well as the constant change of space, we knew that the play was going to be performed by only two actors, Pelicori and Peña again, playing the six characters of the original text. For this, we had a rectangular table covered in a black cloth with two revolving stools at each side. On this table were placed a selection of musical instruments, which the actors used to strengthen the sound aspects of Lorca's beautiful and dark text.

In these performances, whatever the space, and once the call to begin was given, the actors entered the area where the table stood, illuminated by just four lights that were not too bright, greeted the audience like two musicians at a concert, and sat down on the stools. From this moment, the actors began to unfurl the text of this 'erotic hallelujah', changing their voices to transform themselves into the different characters, turning the stools to indicate that there had been a scene change in the story, playing instruments, speaking in unison and employing many other devices; but they never rose from the stools.

A mechanism as simple as two actors seated at a table had one limitation that remained hidden from the eyes of the audience: never, during the course of the whole show, could the actors stand up. We discovered this during a rehearsal: by trying to test out how the actors could increase the size of the area in which they were acting, I asked one of them to leave their seat. When they did, a catastrophe occurred: this erect body, with its vertical lines, exposed the existence of the exterior space. Seated around the table, however, and twisting on their stools, the bodies of the actors made the space function centripetally, with all of the visual lines of their bodies leading towards the table, never upwards, never outwards.

As well as spatial issues, the show was constructed based on a very complex musical idea created by the co-director Edgardo Rudnitzky, an extraordinary musician. Since the spaces we had to perform in did not have reasonable acoustics either (indeed, quite the opposite), we took the decision to use tie-clip microphones subtly to increase the volume of the voices and of some of the instruments. I tend not to have a good relationship with the amplification of voices in the theatre, but in this case the slight increase solved the problem of the concentration of sound, preventing the inevitable dispersal that takes place in spaces that are not acoustically set up for theatre.

Through the objects of the table and the stools, the bodies of the actors and the mics, the mise en scène converged at a central point, cancelling out, in a manner of speaking, the idea of the surrounding space, and thus we could make the show tour an infinity of spaces, not only libraries but also enormous theatres or private living rooms.

This is not always possible. Not all material allows it. Some shows can only be performed in the place where they premiered, others have limited options for being adapted to other spaces. But as long as the idea of the transfer is included in the process of creating the work, the most likely thing is that later, in the various venues where the show is performed, the audience will be able to attend a piece of theatre equivalent to the original. This is a democratic way to conceive of tours. Which is no small thing.

Actors at the centre of the system

For many people in theatre, actors are the centre of the theatre system. Although playwrights will also say that without them theatre would be practically non-existent (in the dressing room at Argentores, the Argentine society of authors, one can read a sign saying 'without a playwright there is no play'), one tends to hear with some insistence that without actors theatre would not exist, and there is a cult of supremacy that performers have over all of the other elements of a mise en scène.

Clearly, this thinking is somewhat limited in that it assumes an idea of theatre in which one element is more important than the others, when it is well known that the performing arts consist in several art forms working simultaneously to form an indivisible whole.

Furthermore, this idea of the actor above all else is somewhat destroyed when one thinks, for example, of the theatre of objects, in which the meaningful thing is precisely the objects that are moved around by the manipulators who may be in view. In this form of theatre there is as much theatre as there would be in a show full of actors' bodies. One might claim that the manipulators are 'actors' but this is not the case, for it is the objects themselves that take this role.

This *ptolomeic* kind of idea that places actors in the centre of the theatrical universe must have appeared and especially been consolidated in recent times for various reasons. One of them, perhaps the most obvious, may be the fact that it is the actors who are in direct contact with the audience at the moment of the performance. The tension that is generated in this encounter between human beings – some in the play and others observing, but both equally alive – can cause those thinking about this phenomenon to forget that there exist many more elements than actors in a mise en scène.

Another possible way of thinking about how such a closed idea may have arisen may have to do with the fact that generally, with the occasional exception, the actors make up the greatest number of people involved in the creation of a show. Unlike in opera, where no one would think of saying 'without singers there would be no opera' (because saying such a phrase would mean flagrantly leaving out the orchestra, the chorus etc.), in the spoken theatre, speaking not of a particular show but of the system in general, the number of actors tends to be much greater than the rest of the people fulfilling other roles. In general there are fewer writers, designers, lighting designers and so on, compared with the number of actors inhabiting theatre circles.

Perhaps the idea of the actor as the only thing necessary for the theatre art spread too as a result of a mistaken reading of the words that open *The Empty Space*, that indispensable book by Peter Brook:

> I can take an empty space and call it a bare stage. A man walks across this empty space whilst someone else is watching him, and this is all that is needed for an act of theatre to be engaged.

This definition has been the source of multiple misunderstandings since it tends to be separated from the sentence that follows, which is the one that takes into account the complexity of the problem:

> Yet when we talk about theatre this is not quite what we mean. Red curtains, spotlights, blank verse, laughter, darkness, these are all confusedly superimposed in a messy image covered by one all-purpose word.[20]

In other words, *theatre*, and with it all of the performing arts, is a complex art form, made up of multiple elements, among which the

---

[20]Brook, Peter, *The Empty Space* (London: Penguin Modern Classics, 2008), p. 12.

actor (or the singer or the dancer) is only one piece of 'material'. If actors can be thought of in their proper place within the mise en scène when one is directing, it is likely that a show can be produced that is powerful because of the strength of all the elements involved. On the other hand, none of this will be possible if the importance of the presence of the actors is exaggerated.

There is no doubt that actors are, in certain circuits, the visible face of the theatre, and for this reason there is a tendency to believe they *are* the theatre. Their faces are the ones on the posters, on the marquees of many of the commercial theatres. It is because of them, some firmly believe, that the audience leave their homes, buy their tickets, go night after night to the theatres and fill them.

But this is only comparatively true. These actors, who appear to be the be-all and end-all of all things theatrical, could not do their work effectively if there were no texts, set, props, costume or all the other elements that make up the totality of the production. Even the most daring of improvisers needs a structure to contain them.

And talking of structures, it should definitely be concluded that there are no 'bad' or 'good' actors per se. The quality of the acting is inescapably linked to the system of the mise en scène that the actors are included in. It is useless for a supposedly good actor to use their expressive resources, and as such their aesthetic ideas, in a system where they do not fit, because an actor has no independence outside of the aesthetic rules expressed in the mise en scène. There are many shows in which some actors do as they please, working more for themselves than for the whole. They delight in their discoveries, in their expressive whims, in those techniques that they find least hard work. And although they succeed in attracting the attention of the audience, it becomes clear that they are not working in the same direction as the rest of the cast, as the music or the space, in other words within the rules set by the mise en scène, causing some chaos – which is not at all interesting – for those watching the show.

Some actors drag out situations unnecessarily, or make eternal self-serving pauses that only bore anyone around them; they delight in small activities that do little to help the audience understand the plot; they whizz over delicate sections of the narrative and disregard the visual or sound aspects of the shows they are performing in.

Many of them are only concerned with their own pleasure, not considering in the least the pleasure of the audience. Others make a cult of 'feeling' onstage, causing the shows to suffer from their temporary moods. And it is well known that when actors 'feel' too much, they involve the audience, and its feelings, less.

I have on occasion had to direct an actor who at no point took the time to look at or above all to understand the set he had to work on. His performance clashed stridently with the visual world of the show and generated an aesthetic imbalance within the mise en scène, a situation which I had in no way intended to happen. Because as an actor he was very well known by the audience from his theatre and television work, most people thought the set was wrong. The set was made up entirely of clean lines, with no decorative shapes whatsoever, a relative absence of colour, and the acting of the rest of the cast corresponded to an idea of expressive sobriety. But in the case of this actor, as a result of the excessive pathos that was unleashed in each of his scenes, above all moving his head and his arms without any sobriety, much of the audience began to long for decorated columns and curtains and believed that the emptiness of the space was a mistake in the show.

I have also worked with actors who were not willing to accept my ideas about the way in which the text we were rehearsing was written. We were dealing with a text filled with effects, littered with traps for the audience, thought out by the writer like clockwork: after so many minutes, another effect to surprise again, and so on. There are many plays like this that fascinate the audience precisely because of the leaps they make and there are writers who know how to do this masterfully. They are plays that appear to be realist but that in fact are not. I thought that the actors ought to be busy trying to work out how to regulate the timings of the entrances and exits of the play's tricks. But the actors argued during rehearsal in favour of trusting their 'feelings' more than the logic of the construction of the text, imposing on their acting something additional that fitted neither the text nor the show: they were trying to act 'truthfully' when there was nothing there but pure artifice.

Fortunately, however, I have also worked with great actors, some of them with a reputation for being divas, those people who in the popular imagination are capricious and do whatever they want with no regard for anything but themselves. Despite this reputation, these actors have in my experience always been the ones who have tried hardest to understand the mechanisms of the mise en scène they are working in. Notably, this kind of actor knows, sometimes without being able to express it in precise words, that they cannot work on their performance without paying attention to all of the aspects included in the mise en scène. They are very aware that it is necessary for all of the elements at play to be at a certain level, in order for them to develop their art. They know that if they share the stage with bad actors, ill-conceived design or defective lighting, this will not make their work look any better.

Only mediocre actors place themselves above everything else, and although they may often convince heedless audiences with their tricks, the truth is that this destroys the *effect of unity* that all shows should have.

Personally, I prefer to work with actors who are capable of thinking about a play as an artistic whole and not from the restricted point of view of the acting alone. The particular system for producing the work does not matter; the actors I tend to work with must have the ability and skill to be able to address the theatrical questions that any complete show needs. Regardless of the material we are working with, they should know that the most important thing is not unleashing their own vanity, the one that believes one can be fine in a show at any price, but rather having an awareness of being part of a show that should have value in all of its elements. I try to steer clear of actors who are only concerned with their own scenes, their own costumes or what light they will have during their appearances, and prefer to stick with those who want to know what the music, the set, their colleagues' costumes or the overall lighting concept of the show are like.

I like working with them because they are intelligent and sensitive, and above all patient. I like knowing that during rehearsals they will let me carry out all the tests that may be needed for making the play, without my having to give too many explanations. Often an idea or an image appears that does not yet have much shape, much less clear words, and that I can only describe as something fuzzy, with a gesture or a stress, but no more than this. This time spent yielding to these first faltering steps allows me to see whether or not the thing I have thought of will work or whether we will have ultimately to abandon it. This does not work with actors who constantly ask why, because they often prevent the unexpected from emerging. On the other hand, those who are trusting, once they have tried something out, can bring their own opinions to the table and will discuss from different points of view, making the work on the mise en scène richer and stronger.

With my favourite actors I can discuss, exchange ideas, argue a lot, negotiate and so on, but ultimately they understand the *collective essence of theatre*, an aspect that many people seem to have forgotten.

The arbitrary and the law

It is hard to know what causes the thoughts which, once activated, turn into works of art, or where it is they come from. There have been various attempts to explain it: aspects of the author's biography, their psychological make-up or as a consequence of the social conflicts and context of the time of creation. Works of art have been treated ad nauseam as the epiphenomenon of causes external to the work of art itself, external to the *logic* of art. But even when these features are *conditioning factors* or *facilitators* of *some* aspects of the work, the truth is that, to date, it has not been possible to know a great deal about the aetiology of the artistic impulse, that moment of revelation, a sort of epiphany, which sets into motion the mechanisms that allow a work of art to be created.

Often, once a work of art is finished, artists try to retrace their steps to reconstruct the path they took to make the work. But, at least in my experience, whenever I try to go back to work out how such-and-such an idea or image was generated, I invariably come up against a void, a gap, a lacuna in my memory of that time before the emergence of those thoughts that shaped the deep structure of the finished work. Seeing that it was impossible to find any rational explanation for the origins of the ideas that drive creation, I came to believe in the power of mystery, which in this case has nothing divine about it, but rather is the place in the psyche that is completely inaccessible until it is released through creativity.

And the truth is that knowing why these thoughts were generated is no longer important. An energy has arisen from the unconscious which mobilizes those who create: something *arbitrary* that expresses the emergence of the new, of the surprising, of the unexpected, of that which lies outside of what is established. Ultimately, the creativity that springs up for no discernible reason.

But from the moment this arbitrary thing appears (not arbitrary in the sense of the capricious, the unjust or the irrational, as tends to be used in social or political matters), the work begins of discovering what its artistic *laws* are. Although the arbitrary thing is creative, it requires *laws* to become a work of art.

It could be said that all artistic work is the interconnection between the arbitrary – those creative impulses that can now be named – and the laws that are generated almost automatically within it, albeit in a way that is not obvious.

Arbitrariness is pure invention, which emerges from mystery; but *artistic laws* are the tools that allow the work of art to be carried out effectively.

In the performing arts the space for searching for and discovering these laws is generally the rehearsals. The daily work of shaping the materials (the space, the acting style, the sounds and so on) begins to reveal how close to or far away from this arbitrary thing one is. The materials used will respond favourably or resist, depending on whether the laws binding the mise en scène together are being met.

And in the search for these laws there are few mysteries. All directors have experienced this, even without knowing they are dealing with a set of laws. When during the rehearsals the director gives indications of acting, rhythm, space and so on, in reality they are setting the rules, that is to say, the laws that the arbitrary thing has generated, which defines what will be allowed into the mise en scène system, and ejects everything that cannot and must not be inside it, what is not useful, what is superfluous. For something to fit well or not into the field of theatre is not a moral question, nor even a cultural one, but rather it comes from considering and accepting as valid the laws that regulate the artistic work on the material. There is no point having brilliant thoughts if, later, when making the show, these laws are not respected.

Why an actor should not turn their back, why that emotion is excessive, why in that moment there is not enough tension between the actors, why the light has to come in in a certain way or why that music is superfluous – these are the manifestation of the specific laws regulating this particular piece of work. Since in the theatre things never have value in of themselves, but rather in relation to each other, in another mise en scène the actor's back may be the most effective thing, excessive emotions might be indispensable for the creation of the scenes, the lack of tension might be adequate for the creation of the relationship between the two characters and the music may need to blast out throughout the entire show.

Recognizing these laws also allows for all of the people who come together for the putting-on of a show to come to reasonably stable agreements, regardless of the discussions being generated. If the subjectivity of the director has not been successfully translated into a kind of 'legal' code, it can give rise to many misunderstandings, as subjectivity in of itself cannot withstand being argued with. And much less can one person challenge another as to whether what they feel is right or wrong. This, as well as being impossible, is above all useless. What can be argued about, however, are the different ways of approaching the material, the different visions that exist about things, and from there, it is likely that the necessary laws will emerge that will allow for a shared code of work.

Perhaps the greatest challenge for a director is allowing oneself to be led by the obvious things that are revealed during rehearsals, those that emerge from the handling of the materials. If the laws being worked with are the correct ones, problems will become apparent and it will be possible to think, correct and modify without any great difficulty. When the material resists and becomes hostile, however, this is probably because the laws relating to the 'something arbitrary', which the material requires, have not been found. In these moments, directors tend to become anxious and intervene with supposed solutions that arise not from the experience of what has been produced, but rather from speculations about what people think they assume that the material ought to be, and in so doing they end up ruining it all a little more. Of course these tensions, these struggles, but above all these upsets become obvious in the final product.

Friction

I belong to a generation and to a cultural milieu for whom theatre, whether one was an artist or an audience member, was an act of passion. One went to the theatre, especially on the independent circuit, to enjoy the art of those who put on the shows, but also one went to be challenged by what one saw and heard in the play, because there was a desire to be 'touched' by the work's themes and aesthetic ideas. Nearly always, after attending a powerful show, there was an almost obligatory time for discussion with one's companions in the cafés near to the venues. Going to the theatre had much political ceremony about it, because as well as attending the shows, and often debating with them, by one's mere presence one was supporting the activity of many of the groups fighting for a truly different space within the city's culture.

Several artistic currents challenged the hegemony of the play from an avant-garde position. There was the realist acting style that was unknown in these parts at that time, supported by the almost violent incursion of the ideas of Stanislavski in the search for 'scenic truth' – theories all read about in books translated from any language except the original Russian, often causing confusion about the use of terms by the followers of these tendencies. There was also a proliferation of mises en scène of Brecht's plays, with their formal breaks in playwriting and acting terms, which dumbfounded the theatrical system and made way for heated discussions about whether one should draw closer to or distance oneself from the audience in order for them to form opinions about the reality that surrounded them. Along other routes walked those who were accused of being agents of 'art for art's sake', that is to

say the de-ideologized kind, when in reality the theatrical forms
were being moulded from other perspectives that would then go on
to transform the work of all theatre practitioners, above all from
the audio-visual point of view.

In all cases, the struggle between the new and the old was
evident; the eternal values of the vanguard became present in each
show that was worthwhile, of course. Every night one went to the
theatre, one expected to see in the play the tension produced by this
contradiction between what had to be left behind and what awaited
us in the future.

In order not to idealize this era too much, I should make it clear
that there was also a lot of bad, ugly theatre, although for those
of us who spent our time arguing about 'the new forms', like the
character of Treplev in Chekhov's *The Seagull*, these shows also
helped us to scrutinize deeply our own approaches when thinking
about the theatre we wanted to make.

Today, ways of thinking about and making theatre have changed.
The contradiction between the new and the old is no longer what
rules the artistic system. The fundamental bases of those vanguards
no longer define the work of theatre artists, because the systems
have become (con)fused with each other. In one single product the
new and the old can coexist without anyone kicking up a fuss about
it. At times, this unsettling tension that mobilized theatre – and art
in general – throughout almost its entire history, but mainly in the
early twentieth century, would seem to have faded away. Only on
some occasions does it unexpectedly appear, not in the shape of
anything new, but in the shape of *friction*. And it is here that theatre
once again becomes an act of wonder.

Friction, this rubbing of one body against a surface to generate
opposing forces, is present in any mise en scène that aims to be
artistic. It generates shock, instability, a particular excitement.
Friction brings the required points of clashing, of tension, of
provocation necessary for the show to be left imprinted on the
memory of the audience.

Friction, like a dull sound that cannot be heard but is always
there, does not allow the audience to be left indifferent as they
watch a show. It may well be that at the end of the performance they
cannot say a word about what has just happened, but somewhere
in their bodies there will be a trace of that indispensable discomfort
that is produced in the presence of art.

Friction is the way that art has to confront and unbalance all those things that are stabilized by culture. Wherever culture sets its rules, friction puts them in doubt. Of all the arts, maybe it is theatre that is most riven with the values that culture constructs, because it is always on a very risky edge, where its expressions can seem to be artistic when in reality they are not. Cultural models, especially those from academic institutions, are increasing invading any nook or cranny that the performing arts leave unguarded, stripping them of their artistic character. In other words, of their profoundly subversive condition.

Artistic vanguards, especially those of the early twentieth century, understood that they were fighting the cultural stability of the bourgeoisie. They battled it with the weapons of art, albeit in an obviously unfair fight. The consequences are those that we can see today, because the fight can no longer be considered in the same terms. Among other reasons (because the subject is beyond the scope of this book), it becomes clear that the capacity for the assimilation of so-called 'new forms' is overwhelming: the contemporary audience of the theatre (and also of other art forms in general – that is, any audience that has a close relationship to the artistic) has become accustomed to receiving any kind of stimulus provoked by a play without necessarily being stirred by what they see and hear.

Friction can be present in many ways: spaces may contradict what one expects from a text; the actors may do something that no one ever expected they would ever do – amidst noisy velocity, provoke an intense silence, an almost impossible void; the scenes may not be seen clearly, the audience may be left to infer them, almost to imagine them. These are just a few examples of friction, which were used in some of the productions that I directed. And in all cases one could foresee that the audience, regardless of their own particular taste, would not be left indifferent.

For theatre to matter, and not to become an increasingly uninteresting ceremony, this artistic disquiet in the audience must continue to be generated.

Furthermore, friction can also be present in any mise en scène in the state-run theatre or in commercial venues, as long as directors know how to apply a level of ingenuity to their work.

Unfortunately, the so-called alternative or fringe theatre, which often claims to be the space where theatre forms are transformed, has often found formulae for writing, acting or space that have left it tremendously stable and no longer surprising practically anyone. Slowly, it is morphing into a kind of theatre that lacks any ability to generate disquiet. As in the tackiest of commercial theatres, the audience already knows what it is going to see and prepares itself not to be surprised. The play that supposedly should be transforming theatre-making offers no tension or friction of any kind to place it in conflict with cultural complacency. It gives the audience *seemingly new forms*, which are neither new nor as unsettling as some theatre artists still think.

Luckily, it is still possible, now and then and almost by surprise, for everything in a place to flee from that horrifying, boring place where culture tries to place the majority of artistic objects. On any kind of stage, some spark of friction may still appear, turning that mise en scène into something exceptional.

It is a case, ultimately, of audiences caring much more about what happens in the play and being happy that they went to the theatre that night, because something unexpected happened to them.